The Bulletproof Leader

Revealing, Realigning, and Restoring the Heart of a Leader

Glenn Dorsey

BroadStreet
P U B L I S H I N G

BroadStreet Publishing® Group, LLC
Savage, Minnesota, USA
BroadStreetPublishing.com

The Bulletproof Leader: *Revealing, Realigning, and Restoring the Heart of a Leader*

978-1-4245-6408-8 (softcover)
978-1-4245-6409-5 (e-book)

Stock or custom editions of BroadStreet Publishing titles may be purchased in bulk for educational, business, ministry, fundraising, or sales promotional use. For information, please email orders@broadstreetpublishing.com.

Design and typesetting | garborgdesign.com

Printed in the United States of America

22 23 24 25 26 5 4 3 2 1

Contents

1

Fight Forward

My heart pounded within my chest. A person I had longed to meet was coming to my place of employment. She whisked into the communications room with a large entourage of people dutifully trailing behind her. She scanned the room and with a confident smile said, "Hello, everyone. My name is Madison." She captivated the room, and she knew it. Madison was the definition of success. She had carved out a business with a net worth in the millions. On the day that I met her, she was scheduled to film a series of miniature commercials to promote her business. Eager to learn from her success, I waited patiently for an opportunity to speak with her.

During the commercials' recording, she was articulate, poised, and persuasive. After she delivered her last line, one of her team members approached her, leaned over, and explained that a small group of people had asked for her autograph. Some hoped for a few minutes of casual conversation. Then a different side of her personality emerged. In a condescending tone, she replied, "I am sure you understand my demanding work schedule. I do not have time to socialize with those who work for me." She grabbed her bag, glared at her assistant, and barked, "We are behind schedule. When are we going to get it together? I do not have time to do my job and yours." Her assistant would not be the only person to whom she spoke with scorn and publicly humiliated that day.

I remember feeling sorry for her staff because Madison's private persona did not resemble her public image, which was encouraging, supportive, and approachable. Behind the scenes, she was rude, rough, and self-absorbed. Looking back, I am thankful that she did not have time for a personal conversation.

Now let's compare Madison to Kate Wynja, a high school senior on the golf team at Sioux Falls Christian School in South Dakota and who won the Class A state golf tournament. She realized later, however, that she had not won at all. In fact, she had made a terrible mistake. On the final hole, a par 5, she posted a four on her scorecard when her actual score was a par 5. She had signed for an incorrect score, and per the rules, disqualification was the result.

Kate made the difficult decision to call a penalty on herself. She reported her mistake to her coach and to tournament officials. It cost her the individual title and cost her team the school's first team title since 2011. Kate apologized to her team for the mistake she had made.[1] She had played by the rules and lost. But Kate understood that it was not about having the best score; it was about everyone playing by the same rules. It was about integrity.

Integrity is taking ownership of our failures, and it means taking responsibility for the damage caused by failure. It's doing the right thing even at the expense of personal loss, as Kate did. Zig Ziglar once said, "Honesty and integrity are essential for success in life—all areas of life. The really good news is that anyone can develop both honesty and integrity."[2] In fact, successful leaders consistently walk in integrity.

When I think of biblical representations of integrity and successful leadership, my mind drifts to the writings of Paul. In one of his letters, he draws an interesting parallel between successful leaders and athletes. He writes:

> Don't you realize that in a race everyone runs,
> but only one person gets the prize? So, run to
> win! All athletes are disciplined in their train-
> ing. They do it to win a prize that will fade away,
> but we do it for an eternal prize. So I run with
> purpose in every step. I am not just shadowbox-
> ing. I discipline my body like an athlete, train-
> ing it to do what it should. Otherwise, I fear
> that after preaching to others, I myself might be
> disqualified. (1 Corinthians 9:24–27 NLT)

In this personal admonition, Paul admitted that he worked hard at holding fast to his integrity as a leader. He owned up to the fact that he had to exert discipline and self-control if he wanted to complete his assignment with honor and uprightness. I have often found confidence in this Scripture passage because I long to complete my journey without negative marks on my record.

My heart is to be a positive influence and an example to those who follow in my footsteps. It's difficult at times, but I crave a level of humility that forces me to find the courage to submit to correction. Like Paul, I want to recognize any fractures that would derail my focus and, if necessary, throw a red flag to call a penalty on my actions. Most of all, I long for the incorruptible crown given to those who firmly fasten their focus on the race set before them. This level of personal awareness and introspection fosters trust and carves out character.

In the ancient book of 2 Kings, we read an obscure but accurate tale about character, and it references a man named Gehazi. Gehazi was selected to serve Elisha, one of the most influential leaders of his generation. If we are honest, it was the kind of opportunity that most leaders in training would kill for. Gehazi was awarded a front seat to some of the greatest miracles in history. It was not unusual for Elisha to bless a woman's barren womb and for that woman to receive the blessing of new life nine months later. It was not surprising when a leper received healing. It was not unheard of when angelic armies appeared out of thin air. It was not extraordinary when Elisha spoke to a dead boy who suddenly stood to attention. Yes, Gehazi had an opportunity that every up-and-coming leader coveted and a position that no one would want to lose.

If we continue to read the book of Kings, we read in the fifth chapter of the second book how a prominent leader named Naaman received healing after following Elisha's prophetic instructions. Desiring to compensate Elisha, Naaman offered him a bountiful reward, including silver, gold, and designer apparel. However, Elisha refused the gesture and sent Naaman on his way. This should be where the story slams shut, but it continues.

In an abrupt turn of events, Gehazi contacted Naaman and set up a covert meeting. Weaving a web of deception, Gehazi managed to obtain all the gifts Naaman had offered Elisha and more. Now read what unfolded when Gehazi met with Elisha:

> When he went in to his master, Elisha asked him, "Where have you been, Gehazi?" "I haven't been anywhere," he replied. But Elisha asked him, "Don't you realize that I was there in spirit when Naaman stepped down from his chariot to meet you? Is this the time to receive money and clothing, olive groves and vineyards, sheep and cattle, and male and female servants? Because you have done this, you and your descendants will suffer from Naaman's leprosy forever." When Gehazi left the room, he was covered with leprosy; his skin was white as snow. (2 Kings 5:25–27 NLT)

Gehazi, one of the most promising talents in the land, not only lost the coveted position but also befell an awful fate. He had charisma but fell short on honor. He lacked the character to handle the power. Gehazi could have been the next Elisha, but he forfeited his future because he lacked integrity.

I remember a comical story that echoes the lesson of Gehazi, and it's been handed down for years. A man came to his friend and asked for prayer because false rumors were being spread about him. The friend told him, "Do not pay any attention to those rumors. Those lies will not hurt you." The man's face went pale as he replied, "But you do not understand; the people telling the lies are about to prove them true." Though fictitious, it's a reminder that our actions catch up to us.

Here's a true story that illustrates the same message. One day a young man knocked on my door. One glance at his troubled face was enough to clue me in that this young man was experiencing great emotional pain. After a cup of coffee, we arrived at the truth: He was disappointed in his pastor, whom he held in great esteem. Over the years, they had developed a deep friendship, and his pastor was like a second father. The young man had never admired a man more than he admired his pastor, and he longed to be just like the man whom he perceived his pastor to be. Simply put, his pastor was his hero.

However, over the last year, he had noticed flaws in his pastor that he could not ignore. A few months before, someone confronted the young man about a back payment his pastor would not settle. At first, he thought there must have been a mix-up. Indeed, there was a reasonable explanation for the confusion. Nevertheless, the pastor's wife later came to the young man, weeping about the financial dilemma their family was facing among a series of questionable, seemingly unethical business decisions her husband had made.

But that was not all. I could tell from the way the young man shifted around in his seat that the most disturbing part of the story was about to unfold. Sure enough, the man discovered that his pastor was cheating on his wife with a lady in the church. As he sat and poured out his grief, I could feel his pain. It wasn't just the pain of another person's failures that he was experiencing; doubts of his mentor's morality began to surface. With a quiver in his voice, he said, "If a man as great as he is can fall, how can I be sure I won't fall as well? How will I ever be able to trust another pastor?"

It's hard to admit, but this kind of occurrence happens more than I want to acknowledge. As Bill Hybels remarked on the chasm between leadership and morality, "People will not follow a leader with moral incongruities for long. Every time you compromise character, you compromise leadership. The foundation of firm leadership is character."[3]

As a young, impressionable pastor, I had a ringside seat to international ministers of influence. I remember admiring one minister so much that I considered resigning from my small church to help him. Then this man whom I admired most made a near-fatal misstep. His moral failure made headlines, and my heart took a hard turn in the opposite direction. I remember standing in front of my television watching a network broadcast when another well-known minister addressed the salacious headlines. His words still echo in my head, "What is wrong with your church? Immorality does not come as a shock to me. Don't you understand these are just men! They are just like you and me, flesh."

Those headlines were not the only ones to ripple through Christianity that year. A handful of other ministers also made costly moral mistakes. Though publicly shamed, several of those men found solid footing in their faith over time. They repented, went through counseling, submitted to authority, and picked up the shattered pieces. Today, their ministries are once again thriving.

When I think of public scandals, my mind lands on Samson, a biblical icon. Samson failed as much as he succeeded. As a leader, he made terrible choices that led him into shameful situations. His involvement with a woman cost him his physical strength, his sight, and his freedom. Enslaved by his adversaries, Samson asked God to give him the strength to win one more battle, and through a sovereign act of mercy, God granted Samson's request. If you have not read through this story in a while (Judges 13–16), I encourage you to do so. You will discover that Samson's final battle was a win of epic proportions.

Just flip on the news or scroll through social media and a list of famous people who have failed will roll across your timeline. In the recent past, a string of politicians and religious leaders have found themselves in courtrooms facing a myriad of civil accusations. Even the FBI has come under scrutiny for falsifying documents to our court system. Influential leaders who appear to be one way in public so often turn out to be the opposite behind closed doors.

The reality is that the human psyche longs for infallible influencers and faultless leaders. Intuitively, we turn ordinary humans into superhumans. We imagine them to be intellectually superior, uniquely gifted, or empowered with a perfect personality. We magnify their strengths and diminish their weaknesses. We convince ourselves that the people we admire possess few or no faults. More often than not, we fail to remember that they, too, are equally flawed, and we're disappointed when they fall short of our expectations.

Leaders are humans, and their failures should not shock us. Failure is a rite of passage for those who succeed. It is the premium for learning by experience. Those who think success stories do not include failure need to consider The University of Southern California's School of Cinematic Arts, which rejected Steven Spielberg not once but twice.[4] He would later produce movies that grossed more than $9 billion and earn three Academy Awards. Walt Disney is another failure-to-fame story. A newspaper editor fired him, criticizing his drawings and claiming they "lacked imagination."[5] Today Walt's enterprise is valued at $165 billion. Oprah Winfrey was fired from her first job in television but later became a billionaire who owns a television network. Although some leaders may seem like overnight sensations, the truth is that their beginnings are often messy.

Let's revisit the Bible, specifically the middle of the book of John, where we read another story of seemingly messy beginnings. Jesus learned that his good friend Lazarus had died. Four days later, Jesus arrived at the burial site, and Lazarus's family complained that Jesus was too late. Jesus locked eyes on them and proclaimed that he was right on schedule. When others thought Lazarus's life had ended, Jesus knew it was just the beginning. In a loud voice, Jesus commanded those in charge to remove the stone that sealed the tomb. You can imagine the mockery and critical accusations hurled his way. Nevertheless, they followed his instructions. Now pay close attention to what happened next: "Jesus shouted, 'Lazarus, come out!' And the dead man came out, his hands and feet bound in graveclothes, his face wrapped in a headcloth. Jesus told them, 'Unwrap him and let him go!'" (John 11:43–44 NLT).

As we think through this scene, we can see that Jesus went out of his way to rescue Lazarus. By removing the lid from the tomb, Jesus did away with every obstacle that would prevent Lazarus from hearing his voice. He called him out of the dark place that had the word *death* stamped all over it. However, even with all that Jesus did, Lazarus still had to initiate faith steps and walk out of the grave. The same is true in our lives. If we want Jesus to rescue us, we have to do our part to separate ourselves from things holding us captive.

Now, let us consider one last thing before we wrap up the story of Lazarus. When John communicates this story, he intentionally includes that although Lazarus walked out of the grave, he remained bound in burial cloths. That one detail should make us go silent with wonder. He was alive but still bound. Maybe that describes your situation in some way. There are parts of your life that are fully alive and other parts that you know need freedom. In a caring way, Jesus told the disciples to "Unwrap him and let him go!" Jesus was not satisfied that his friend was alive.

He wanted to unravel the things that kept Lazarus bound so that he could walk freely.

God is not just merciful to people named Samson. He is equally invested in you and me. The grace he gave Samson is the same grace he longs to give to you. He is equally as passionate about rescuing us and helping us walk in freedom as he was with Lazarus.

Maybe you are in a place of failure. Perhaps your situation didn't make headlines, but it rocked your world nonetheless. Let me encourage you, for at one time or another, we have all found ourselves slipping away from solid ground. Whether our indiscretions made seismic waves or slight ripples, the path to recovery is the same. In times of failure, we must reach for repentance, restoration, and reconciliation.

Over the years, I have tried to understand why some leaders fall at the first round of fire and why others seem ethically immune to failure. After wrestling with this question, I've come to understand that the answer—the common denominator among these failures—can be traced back to a lack of personal accountability and transparency. If we are unconscious of and unwilling to own up to our vulnerabilities, weaknesses, or character flaws, then they destroy us over time. That's why the practice of safeguarding our souls must be a priority, not an act of penance.

I personally admire leaders who take care of issues on the front end rather than waiting for the situation to become a crisis. And trust me, leaders who care about their relationships and reputations proactively shield what matters most to them, including their spouses, their ministries, and their jobs. I recently read an article that revealed that former vice president Mike Pence refuses to eat alone with a woman or attend an event where alcohol is served unless his wife is present. As soon as this news dropped, critics mocked his boundary and went so far as saying that his actions could be a violation of anti-discrimination laws.[6] Seriously. Imagine that someone would be brazen enough to pursue legal action against a high-profile leader because he would not put himself in a compromising situation.

We cannot be too cautious when leading from a place of authenticity and transparency. If you want to get serious about protecting yourself from weakness that could unravel your life, I encourage you to master accountability. Be open and responsible in your relationships. Keep a record of your conversations. Let others know your whereabouts. Moreover, be transparent enough to honestly answer questions that relate to your integrity and proudly show that you have nothing to hide.

My purpose in writing this book is to draw out the greatness hidden within you. This is not a book to teach the principles of leadership or how to be a better leader. It is to help make the leader better—bulletproof. The bulletproof leader walks in absolute confidence of their identity. They are impervious to critics who do not accept them. They live an open, transparent life. They have no fear of a successful attack on their character because maintaining their character is more important to them than maintaining their job. The bulletproof leader leverages their failures as lessons that help them become even better. Their conscience is clear. They surround themselves with people who add to whatever they may lack in their life. They are free to be themselves. They are unstoppable.

As we journey through this book, I trust you will begin to see the benefits of leading an authentic and transparent life. I believe the truths within each chapter will empower you to live above reproach and without regret. I believe we are stronger when we refuse to be anyone other than who we indeed are.

Our assignment in life, our personal calling, and our influence are important to the One who created us. He does not simply look at our struggles; he looks at the positive situations that can come from them. If you are willing to be honest and transparent, God will highlight areas of your life in need of transformation. He has not changed his mind about you or the purpose he has for your life. God held your future long before you made your first mistake or took that near-fatal fall. If you find yourself in need of grace, reach out and allow God to write an epic ending into your story. Fight forward and regain whatever you might have lost.

2

Love the People You Lead

I stood behind a large podium and spoke to a full audience. Halfway through my presentation, I looked down and made a startling discovery: My pants were missing. I couldn't imagine why. Panic set in as a thousand questions flashed through my mind. How could I have forgotten to put on pants? How was I going to get out of the room without someone seeing me? More importantly, what would people think of me? The audience appeared oblivious, so I continued to speak. As I approached the end of my presentation, desperation overcame my emotions. I jolted awake, and it took a few moments for me to realize that my nightmare was nothing more than a tormenting scenario of my subconscious imagination. If you have ever had a nightmare that was hard to shake, you understand the nature of what I experienced that night. I admit I had to down a few cups of coffee to subdue my feelings from the dream.

Over the years, I have read studies that conclude that our unsettling dreams often stem from anxiety and the feeling of being unprepared for something that looms in the future. Oddly, my nightmare reminded me of the story of the first man and woman. If we were to dust off the first ancient book of Genesis, we would read how their real-life experience was not all that different from my nightmare.

Long before Adam and Eve found themselves in a mess, God warned them not to eat from the Tree of Knowledge of Good and Evil. But instead of following God's instructions, they took unwise counsel from something, or rather someone, with a sinister plan. If you read the story closely, you will discover that Eve followed the serpent's suggestion and ate from the forbidden tree. And she didn't stop with her own indulgence either; she convinced her husband to follow in her footsteps. With one bite of the forbidden fruit (and just like my nightmare), the couple suddenly stood naked before all of creation (Genesis 3).

Before we get too far ahead of ourselves and journey down a winding theological road that may lead us off track, let's retrace our steps to the beginning of their story. Before their fall in the garden, they walked with God unclothed and unashamed. They were unconscious of their condition because they were spiritually clothed and without sin. No sin meant no shame. The only covering they needed was the concealment of God's glory.

Imagine what it must have been like to live in paradise. If you have time, take a moment and allow your senses to soak in

If we are to experience freedom + embrace life in full measure, we must accept who God created us to be + give others the freedom to be who God made them. We must only feel a true sense of peace + wholeness that we are on the inside.

the fragrance of the flowers. Follow the gently trek through the valley. Watch in lope along together. Before you let your imagination wander too far, consider the one thing missing from this utopia. Have you figured it out? The thing that separated their world from ours is *death*.

Death stings. Death steals. Death destroys. When death entered the world, so did dishonor. Consider that before sin ushered in shame, the first couple could freely stand naked before the world. They were comfortable with the conditions of their created purpose. Living in a state of innocence, they felt holy. They *were* holy. Being mentally, physically, and emotionally whole, they embraced their identity without a trace of insecurity.

I have counseled leaders of various organizations over the years. After spending time with them and observing their strengths and weaknesses, I often discover that many of them share a common personal struggle, which is the very same one that Adam and Eve came to struggle with in their own way. The underlying problem of the leaders I worked with is that they find it hard to be authentic versions of themselves apart from the pressures and demands of their careers.

If we are to experience freedom and embrace life in full measure, we must accept who God created us to be. We must also give others the freedom to be who God made them. If we are not comfortable enough to embrace our identity, why would we place that burden or expectation on others? We can only lift others up to the level of wholeness that we are on the inside. That is, a foundational stone for effective leadership is identity.

I will never forget Dr. Myles Munroe sharing on the topic of understanding one's identity in Christ: "You don't have to try to be somebody, because you are somebody."[7] Because identity is the foundation of confidence, Adam and Eve gained their identity from daily fellowship with God. The writer of Genesis documents the details this way:

> The eyes of both were opened, and they knew that they were naked. And they sewed fig leaves together and made themselves loincloths. And they heard the sound of the Lord God walking in the garden in the cool of the day, and the man and his wife hid themselves from the presence of the Lord God among the trees of the garden. (Genesis 3:7–8 ESV)

After they ate the forbidden fruit, they lost their innocence and their identity. The intimate times they had with God would never be the same. They would never be comfortable unclothed in his presence. They found themselves hiding, afraid to be seen by God. Man became self-conscious instead of God-conscious.

Before Adam and Eve's act of disobedience, *naked* referred to innocence and openness. The term changed to mean "uncovered, revealed, or exposed" after their encounter with evil. As toddlers, we had no inhibitions being naked. However, as we came of age, to be naked took on feelings of self-consciousness. Shame. Violation. Guilt. Vulnerability.

When we find ourselves uncovered, we instinctively reach for something to conceal our bareness. Just like the first couple, we pray fervently that others will not notice. When we face humiliation and are disappointed with our actions, we shy away from God's presence. And just like Adam, we try to cover our tracks and conceal our shortcomings.

As I think back over the story, I wonder why Adam and Eve covered themselves with fig leaves. Fig leaves can only grow as large as five inches wide and ten inches long. For all practical purposes, these withering fig leaves would not last long. To remain covered, they would have to replenish the foliage daily if not every few hours.

When we are disappointed in our behavior, we often try to right things by covering our tracks. And like Adam and Eve, our efforts only exhaust us. Our feeble attempts to replace the glory of God leave us lacking and lonely. Remember, whenever we exalt our will above God's, we become insubordinate and uncovered. Pride and disobedience only lead to one place: a dusty dead end.

Anyone who's studied history remembers a particular leader whose charisma captured the heart of a nation. He was persuasive enough to convince most of his peers that his ideology of a supreme race was factual, not flawed. His eloquent speeches spoke to a nation that longed for change and felt torn apart by crisis. But behind that confident façade was an issue he didn't want others to see. He would occasionally shuffle his feet or tug at one leg that lagged behind the other when he walked. If you looked closely, then you might have noticed that he kept one hand tucked in his back pocket or shoved inside his coat, for he feared others might see his secret: The chancellor of Germany, Adolf Hitler, had Parkinson's disease.[8]

Another world leader gave speeches that brought courage to a troubled nation. Because he was rarely photographed, most of the historical images capture him sitting at a desk or standing behind a podium. The effects of childhood polio limited his ability to walk. The man was Franklin Roosevelt, the thirty-second president of the United States.

Like these great leaders, we often go out of our way to avoid drawing attention to our weaknesses. And honestly, those efforts to hide our flaws can leave us feeling worn out and weary. We expend unnecessary energy trying to camouflage our moral crashes. And just like Adam and Eve, the discovery of our flaws will often send us running to isolate. The truth is that nothing changes until we deal with our flesh. We must come out of hiding and into a place of healing.

In the heart of almost everyone is the desperate desire to be accepted. Not to be validated for *what* we do but accepted for *who* we are. To be recognized and received even when we stray or sink beneath massive mistakes. We search for grace in our soul that will let us grow from and beyond our faults and failures.

Over Sunday lunch, a man named Matt met with Kevin, a senior pastor of fifty years. When Matt first started preaching, it was Kevin who allowed him to speak at his church. Their history was long and their friendship deep. During lunch, Kevin reached into the vault of his life experiences and shared some secrets with Matt. Every story that Kevin shared was unique, and every word carried the weight of wisdom. At times Matt could feel the emotional tension as Kevin paused to make sure he spoke only what

God wanted him to share. Oddly, it seemed as though Kevin was speaking from his past into Matt's future: "Matt, someday you will pastor a church where people will accept you for who you are. They will lovingly receive you and not try to change you. The population of the city or the size of the church will not matter. When you find *that* church, stay and don't leave."

The heaviness of Kevin's words lingered in the restaurant long after they had left. Fifteen years later, Matt found the place to which Kevin was referring. It was the smallest city he had ever pastored in before, but the people accepted him—flaws and all. Pastoring that small congregation of people who received him, not just his calling, afforded him the opportunity for personal growth. Matt, in time, was able to create a vision for the church and community. As he grew in wisdom, the church grew in numbers. Both succeeded.

One of the struggles many leaders face is not having enough tenure to establish a vision. Leaders are continually contending for time. Time to develop meaningful relationships. Time to fulfill demanding deadlines. Time to perform. Time to produce. Many leaders feel an internal metronome of anxiety. They sense the urgency behind every expectation. The clock becomes a pressure cooker, inside of which leaders are evaluated and often replaced. A recent poll from Lifeway Research revealed the average pastor's tenure in a local church is 3.6 years. Studies are suggesting that for effective leadership to develop, between 11.2 to 21.6 years are needed.[9]

It is widely known that long-term leaders are more effective and tend to thrive in the organizations they lead. Their success is often related to the fact that they have gained the trust of their followers. Members are familiar with the leader's achievements, and they trust his or her judgment. They have bought into the leader's vision and are willing to carry it out.

Another interesting observation is that when leaders have shorter tenures than board members, a disruption of the organization's vision may occur because of the change. A new director may aspire to change the mutually agreed upon vision cast by the preceding director and board.

I have pastored four churches. I only stayed at my first church for eighteen months, the second four years, the third five years, and the last church for thirty-three years. I am ashamed to admit that I did not have a vision for the congregations while pastoring the first three churches. The reason is that I did not stay long enough for my leadership to establish a defined vision.

Acceptance grows over time as one learns to build relationships that are open, honest, and real. When we are honest about our faults and failures, we become transparent with others and ourselves. The transparency of Paul the Apostle allows us to see him as human and not some super-saint. I have learned that by being open with our struggles, we allow others to perceive us as authentic and believable. In an inexplicable way, vulnerability often increases our influence.

Authentic leaders are willing to contribute more than just their talents; they give themselves to those they serve. A leader goes beyond the surface of mind-to-mind communication by communicating heart to heart, spirit to spirit. And that often requires some degree of releasing control.

For many years, I traveled to Ireland to do ministry work. On one flight to Dublin, I asked the Holy Spirit if he wanted me to share anything in particular with the people. Without hesitation, I felt him whisper, "I want you to teach on the topic of control." I responded with the excuse that I had never read or taught on the topic. Before the flight was over, the Holy Spirit gave me four characteristics of a controlling spirit and how those characteristics would negatively affect the striving for control. The following paragraphs lay out four toxic habits around power and control that leaders should avoid.

Controlling leaders lose peace when they are not in control. If you were to read through the first book of Samuel, you would find a king by the name of Saul. If you are familiar with his story, you know how evil spirits tormented him. Most theologians would agree that his fits of rage, moments of madness, and conspiracy theories were byproducts of his pride and arrogance. His home, to put it bluntly, was a house of horrors. He manipulated his daughters and blackmailed his sons. Not once but five times Saul attempted to kill David. He even went the distance to control the prophet of the nation. Saul was equal parts manipulator and a man gone mad. The one who wanted to be in control was the one spinning out of control.

My friend Pastor Goins counseled a woman experiencing marriage troubles. He attempted to convince her that she had severe control issues. He told her, "You are such a controller that when your husband is driving, you tell him when the light is red or green. You remind him of the speed limit. You tell him when to stop, go, and turn."

She responded, "That is true! He drives me nuts with his reckless driving. I wish I had a steering wheel on my side of the car."

"Thank you," he told her. "You've made my point." Granted, not every back seat driver has control issues, but this illustration was what she needed in order to understand how she was destroying the peace in her family.

Controlling leaders create angry, resentful followers. Leaders who make all the decisions strip away the will of others. Consider this imaginary scenario: A man called his wife and said, "Baby, tonight, I am taking you on a date. Dress your best and choose any restaurant you want. I'll pick you up at five o'clock."

His wife was ecstatic as she imagined the romantic night out. As planned, he arrived on time and escorted her to the car. As they drove away, he leaned over, touched her hand, and asked, "Where do you want to have dinner?"

She responded, "I would love to go to Hugo's. I am in the mood for good Italian food."

Immediately he cut her short and said, "Oh no! I had lunch there today. Let's try Monty's Steakhouse."

If you were the wife in this situation, how would you feel? Her enthusiasm shot out the door before he had time to close it. The moment he took away her ability to choose was the instant he snatched away her joy. Without realizing his mistake, he sabotaged the evening and sowed seeds that could reap a harvest of anger and resentment.

Now let's consider why he didn't let her make a choice. Why did he give her the option to choose and then retract it? Perhaps the answer is pride. Pride often encourages us to exert our will over someone else's. Pride was the sin of Adam and Eve, and it is the same type of injustice that makes followers despise their leaders.

Controlling leaders suppress the identities of others. When I think about this point, my mind immediately goes to the ancient writings of the prophet Daniel. In the first chapter of Daniel, he recounts the story this way: "Among these were Daniel, Hananiah, Mishael, and Azariah of the tribe of Judah. And the chief of the eunuchs gave them names: Daniel he called Belteshazzar, Hananiah he called Shadrach, Mishael he called Meshach, and Azariah he called Abednego" (Daniel 1:6–7 ESV).

The men listed here found themselves slaves of a foreign nation. When they became slaves, it wasn't just their surroundings that changed; their names changed as well. When they arrived in Babylon, King Nebuchadnezzar threw their native names out the window. The move was both poignant and political. He changed their names, diet, clothes, and language. This seemed to be a common practice among conquering kings who wanted to break down the identities of their captives. A similar tale is spun in the book of Genesis when a king changed Joseph's name to Zaphenath-paneah. Granted, leaders of today lack the authority to change peoples' names, but they can pressure them to change their identity. The need to control people's actions and reactions isn't always a measure of management; many times, it is a sign of complete control.

Over the years I have learned that pride isn't just a sign of arrogance; sometimes it's a sign of those who are hurting. When people are deeply wounded or rejected, they often create emotional barriers between themselves and the rest of the world. Too often, those barriers block out the very people who can and want to help them heal. They hide behind emotional walls because they don't want anyone to sense or know their pain. Instead of relationships growing deeply, they remain shallow and distant.

We are never more unlike Jesus than when we hide behind self-made walls or exclude people from our world. We cannot reject others simply because we fear rejection. Though rejected by humanity, Jesus threw out the net and said, "Come...whosoever will, let him take the water of life" (Revelation 22:17 JUB), and "He that comes to me I will in no wise cast out" (John 6:37 JUB).

I've met many leaders who emotionally withdraw at the moment that they should go *all in*. As a reminder, Jesus was an *all-in* type of leader. He was accepting and accessible. If we are to lead humankind, we must resemble humanity. The created purpose of leadership is to make us inclusive, not to keep us lonely.

Nothing will change in our life until we are willing to tear down the walls of our insecurities. When we feel threatened, we are quick to throw up bricks of resistance. Before long, we barricade ourselves off from danger, and protection turns into pride. We look as foolish as Adam and Eve, hiding behind the fig leaves of our human conceit.

Controlling leaders run from intimacy. If you asked most men to define intimacy, they would probably say "sex." Ask women to explain the same term, and you will likely hear answers like "hugs, kisses, snuggling, and affirming words." Although these are indeed ways that people express love, they are not examples of intimacy. Intimacy is when someone knows and accepts us for who we are.

In today's world, people wear emotional fig leaves. Married couples share a home, children, money, and their bodies, but not their inner feelings. They fear that if they reveal the truth, then their spouses might use it against them. They anticipate the reaction and conclude that the potential consequences are not worth the risk.

After months of guilt, my friend Jillian's husband decided to confess the truth and make a clean start. Over dinner one night, he told his wife about his pornography addiction. As imagined, Jillian didn't take the news well. She lit into him, spouting off a series of questions and expletives: "What's wrong, my body? Do I not make you happy? Why would you want to look at another woman when you have me? Do you know how that makes me feel? You are sick."

After a few days, Jillian calmed down. She tried to look at things from her husband's perspective. Yes, he messed up. He also admitted his failure. He didn't have to risk telling her, but he trusted her enough to be open and honest. She was still angry, but she saw his remorse and knew he was genuinely sorry for hurting their marriage.

Later that week, she approached him again: "I know you never intended for things to end up like this. I know that you confessed your addiction to me because you love me and want my help. I am hurt, but I forgive you. I know it won't be easy, but

I believe that we can overcome this." Intimacy is choosing to love someone despite his or her faults, sins, or weaknesses.

Many times, I have heard leaders confess they can only serve people by keeping them at arm's length. After being a pastor all these years, I know why they say that. They have been hurt and don't want to experience that kind of hurt again. But the truth is that when we shut ourselves off from people, we come across as callous and unapproachable.

To be a servant leader, we must love the people we lead. Only then will our influence change those whom we serve. We must give them our hearts, knowing not only that we will hurt again but also that love and intimacy are the rewards of investing ourselves in the lives of other people.

3

Submit to God's Authority

Leaders are expected to develop their strengths and minimize or ignore their weaknesses. They are encouraged to improve whatever they're good at and discouraged from sweating "the small stuff." I take exception to this skewed logic. Not paying attention to our weaknesses can lead to catastrophic consequences.

After admitting he had gambled on baseball games during the time he managed a major league team, Pete Rose was banned from the game for life, and the baseball commissioner declared him ineligible for inclusion in the Hall of Fame.[10] As one of the highest-paid athletes of his era, it is hard to imagine that he would risk his reputation and successful career on a simple bet. One has to wonder what he was thinking and when his gambling addiction began. I don't know the answer to either question, but it is possible that one winning bet turned into two, and the rush of winning produced a high that was hard to shake. More often than one might imagine, addictions that start small don't stay small.

Like the unnoticed ripple of waves preceding a tsunami, no one pays attention until the tidal wave makes landfall. Take the collapse of the Silver Bridge for example. Spanning the Ohio River, the 55-foot aluminum suspension bridge was more than forty years old when it suddenly collapsed in mid-December of 1967. Thirty-two vehicles crossing the bridge at the time dropped into the river below. Forty-six people died, and two bodies were never recovered. Investigators examined the wreckage and discovered that a 0.1 inch crack hidden deep in one of the bridge's metal bars, aggravated by years of heavy traffic and poor maintenance, caused the catastrophic failure that brought the bridge down in the middle of rush hour traffic.[11]

A leader with serious character flaws is like the metal bar that broke the bridge. People crossing the bridge had confidence in the builders, but because the defect was hidden below the surface, forty-six people lost their lives. Slight mistakes can have colossal consequences. To add emphasis to this logic, let's revisit the garden of Eden:

> When the woman saw that the tree was good
> for food, and that it was a delight to the eyes,
> and that the tree was to be desired to make one
> wise, she took of its fruit and ate, and she also

gave some to her husband who was with her,
and he ate. (Genesis 3:6 ESV)

Eve defied the command of God, which was to not eat from the Tree of Knowledge of Good and Evil. If you are like me, you may agree that taking a bite of fruit doesn't seem like a significant offense. I would have filed Eve's actions under the misdemeanor rather than in the felony column. Why such an uproar over a bite of fruit? Isn't that the way we view our sins—as a minimum not a maximum offense? We reason that lustful thoughts shouldn't land us in the same lineup with the adulterers. Taking credit for work that isn't ours shouldn't square us away with the Bernie Madoffs of our generation. I'm sure this abatement of action line of thinking is how Eve expected God to view her behavior. He didn't. The truth is that one small sin brought havoc and death to the entire human race.

Temptation is a part of life. It demands a *Yes, I will* or a *No, I would never* kind of response. Sometimes, those with little to lose influence our reaction to temptation. In the garden, the serpent had nothing at stake. His reputation wasn't on the line, and no one depended on him to make the right choice or do the right thing. But Adam and Eve stood to lose everything. As they would learn, one misguided decision would determine their destiny and all of humanity's.

Adam and Eve had dominion over the earth. They lived in the perfect utopia and were given authority to rule everything in creation. In today's world, we would consider them to be among the elite, possessing wisdom, wealth, power, and prosperity. Why would they risk losing everything? They gambled because they longed for the forbidden. They gambled and lost. In an instant, the well-watered garden became a wasteland. Panic replaced peace. Prosperity turned into poverty. A single decision to disregard the Creator's instruction locked them out of paradise forever.

We need to keep in mind that small choices shape our destiny in ways we cannot imagine. After the deconstruction of a crisis, the truth is that an average leader can figure out the mistakes. However, a prudent leader will avoid missteps before taking them. The wise man Solomon said, "The prudent gives thought to his steps" (Proverbs 14:15 ESV). Refuse to be the leader who doesn't see what is at stake until it is too late to recover.

My heart aches when I hear stories of how once-trusted employees make a series of bad decisions and find themselves dismissed from their job. Even worse is when what started as a minor infraction eventually costs someone their respected name. If we are to hold fast to our reputations and live as ethical leaders, we must identify the areas where we are most vulnerable. Everyone has an area of weaknesses that could lead to failure. And I'm not referring to small slip-ups but the kinds of liability that, if left unchecked, could reduce us to ruin. A wise leader recognizes that it can lead to their downfall if they ignore a fault over time.

When I consider great leaders who struggled with personal issues, my thoughts immediately drift to Moses. Most forget that at age 40, Moses killed a man and buried his body. That clip of his highlight reel plays more like a scene from *The Godfather* than the Bible. And just like any action-packed drama, an act of unchecked anger left Moses narrowly escaping the king's sword. Isn't that what sin does? It places us on the defensive side of life.

Moses went from being a member of the royal family to living like a nomad in the wilderness. For forty years, he looked after sheep. And trust me, nothing is quite as humbling as staring at a flock of filthy sheep day in and day out. Over time, the haughtiness he felt was replaced by the humility he learned in the wilderness. I'm sure we've all had our share of experiences that took our pride down a notch or two.

During this rough patch of life, God called Moses to return to Egypt and lead two and a half million people away from the dictator's régime. I'm not sure that this is what Moses had in mind. I'm not sure he liked leading sheep, but I'm quite sure he didn't want to lead the people of Israel. As I have researched histories of great leaders, I've stumbled upon a secret: Great leaders aren't always the confident ones. Sometimes they are just the *called* ones. Moses started as a below-average leader, and it took four decades for him to evolve into a great leader.

I've often thought it ironic that Moses delivered a nation but never found deliverance for himself. The same anger management issue that compelled him to murder an Egyptian in his twenties is the same uncontrolled anger that kept him out of God's promises in his eighties. When God instructed Moses to strike the rock once to draw forth water for his people, Moses, angry at the rebellion of the Israelites, struck the rock twice (Numbers 20:10–11). If you have ever served a leader who flies into a rage, you know the irreparable harm they inflict upon others and themselves. When tempted to act out in anger, I meditate on this Scripture verse: "A man without self-control is like a city broken into and left without walls" (Proverbs 25:28 ESV).

Over the years, I have discovered that an angry leader seldom produces motivated followers. While anger may help them release pent-up frustrations, it drives those who witness their fury to pull away. Although I can't entirely agree with all of Buddha's mantras, I wholeheartedly agree with this one: "Holding on to anger is like grasping a hot coal with the intent of throwing it at someone else; you are the one who gets burned."

A person who is out of control is never in control. I've watched angry men pound their fists and women scream and shout. I've never witnessed a raging person earn respect. An angry outburst usually generates the opposite reaction of what one might imagine. A friend once said, "If you want to win the case, don't force your adversary to lie; just get them to sound angry when they tell the truth." When a leader reacts in unchecked anger, it is clear that fear and failure are imminent.

As a child, I remember being fascinated by the story of Jonah. The account of a man swallowed by a gigantic fish and then vomited out of its belly is the kind of tale boys love to read. After revisiting Jonah's story as an adult, I see that Jonah's principal problem wasn't a sea serpent but rather the prophet's inability to follow God without resenting his instructions. Jonah was a quick trigger kind of guy when it came to anger.

We discover that Jonah's rage stemmed from not wanting to follow God's instructions concerning the city of Nineveh. In short, the Ninevites were the enemy of Jonah's people. God was looking for a man who would extend mercy. Jonah didn't want

God to save them; he wanted God to eradicate them. Jonah was looking for a way out. In an ironic turn of events, by the time Jonah's story wraps up, it is Jonah, not the Ninevites, who finds himself estranged from God. As I've come to learn, displaced anger is the first step down the long road of regret.

I learned a tough lesson about hair-triggers through hunting, one of my favorite hobbies. I have hunted a variety of game in my lifetime. But bird hunting, such as pheasant, chucker, quail, dove, or ducks, is my favorite. I love following trained dogs who trail the birds, pose on point when they find them, and retrieve the bird after I hit the mark. It is a constant action sport. My father, an avid hunter, meticulously taught me the rules of firearm safety at an early age. We never loaded our firearms until we were in the field. When we stored our guns, we left the chambers open. Part of my father's instructions were to have respect for weapons and to fear their potential danger.

It was a family tradition on Thanksgiving Day to have a quail hunt before the festive meal. On one of these special hunts, my father, some other family members, and I hunted around a local lake. We had flushed a covey of quail that had scattered in a wooded area. I was unfamiliar with the shotgun I was using that day. Because there were more hunters than usual, a shot quicker than normal was required. I was among the youngest in the group, and I wanted to make an impression.

The dogs went on point, and we were all positioned for a shot. The bird was airborne and turned behind my father. Being unfamiliar with the gun I was using, I didn't know it had a hair-trigger, requiring only the least touch to discharge. Aiming at the bird in flight, I touched the trigger, and it fired before I was ready. My father yelled and put his hands over his ears. I was overwhelmed with fear thinking I had shot him. Thank God I had not. But the shot was so near his head that his hearing was affected by the explosion. Needless to say, I learned to beware the hair-trigger.

Similar to the way a hair-trigger is set to release given the slightest pressure, so, too, is anger ready to explode out of our emotional chamber under the least amount of tension. Just like the spray of a shotgun, explosive outrage can hit people we never intend to harm. As leaders, it is our responsibility to keep our emotions from blasting away at innocent bystanders.

I had a friend named Mark who was notorious for losing his temper. After an outrage, he would feel guilty and pretend that nothing had happened. Over time his rage worsened, and his remorse lessened. It wasn't long before his colleagues avoided him, and his family resented him. More often than we realize, our attitudes distance us from the people and positions we crave most. If we want to live out our days in peace and fulfillment, we must ask ourselves difficult questions: What personal weakness could paralyze our potential? What unguarded emotion would our enemy use to dismantle our dreams? A mistake cost Mark a promotion. An outburst of anger locked Moses out of the promised land. What aspiration could your weakness snatch right out of your hand?

God doesn't justify our mistakes because we are the chief influencers in an organization. When God scolded Moses for his angry outburst, Moses dared to blame his followers. I've watched similar tantrums from leaders on their social media feeds. Those who should be diffusing a social fight are often the ones initiating it. As leaders, we can't always avoid being the subject of public jabs, but we can be mindful of how we respond to them. The enemy of our soul is waiting to make a mockery of our weakness. Like a lion on the prowl, the enemy waits for us to reach our highest level of influence before he takes a swipe at our soul. He lurks in our blind spots and hides in the dark places of our hearts. Like a good scavenger, he searches for signs that we are faltering or failing to keep in step with what we know is right.

Maybe you are weary or struggling with difficult situations. In your weariness, trust your experience. You have been here before, and you will be again. The prize always goes to the one who finishes the race. Endurance is an excellent developer of character. To be a leader requires mental toughness. One more day of moving forward. One more day of focusing on your goal. Determination will reach down inside you and create a picture of you standing in the winner's circle. Yes, you are a finisher.

Muhammad Ali is an excellent example of how dedication and discipline will accelerate natural abilities. Ali's trainer, Angelo Dundee, taught him to be "the greatest of all time." Ali recognized that if he were to be the world's heavyweight champion, he would have to think and train like a title weight holder. When asked how he felt about his workout regimen, he replied, "I hated every minute of training, but I said, 'Don't quit. Suffer now and live the rest of your life as a champion.'"[12] He was willing to battle feelings of fatigue to boast the belt of a champion. If we are to lead successfully, like Ali, we must learn to submit our gifts to a superior trainer's supervision and instruction.

Throughout biblical history, great leaders learned to submit their potential to God's authority. Assuming the responsibility of a nation was overwhelming to Solomon, the son of David. David gave him plans, finances, and materials to build an elaborate temple (1 Chronicles 28: 9–21). Overwhelmed with the assignment, he knew he needed God's help. In a dream, God appeared to Solomon and asked him what wanted. Aware of his need, he asked for understanding to discern and judge people. Solomon trusted God with his potential and submitted to his authority. Because Solomon asked wisely, God honored him: "God gave Solomon very great wisdom and understanding, and knowledge as vast as the sands of the seashore" (1 Kings 4:29 NLT). Wisdom, understanding, and knowledge are necessary for accelerated promotion as a leader.

I often hear talk among leaders about taking their ministry or business to the next level. I understand what they mean, but I'm not sure that they know how much sacrifice comes with it. The higher a leader climbs up the ladder, the greater the risk of a fatal fall. Should that risk discourage us from pursuing our dreams? No, but it should make us more mindful of securing our steps lest our feet slip.

With greater influence comes greater responsibility. We must be responsible enough to rid ourselves of whatever issues may bar us from our destiny. Numerous times in Scripture, small things bring to ruin things of great value. Little foxes spoil vineyards (Song of Solomon 2:15). A little yeast destroyed the whole lump (1 Corinthians 5:6). A little lust brings forth ruin (1 Timothy 6:9), and "a little folly outweighs wisdom and honor" (Ecclesiastes 10:1 ESV).

It is easy to get caught up in our weaknesses and convince ourselves that what we are doing is somehow acceptable. In King Solomon's book, he made a profound statement regarding transgressions that go unpunished: "When a crime is not punished quickly, people feel it is safe to do wrong" (Ecclesiastes 8:11 NLT).

I will be the first to admit that it is easy to justify our sins when we are not ready to give them up. Just ask anyone who has found themselves in a self-made mess. Whenever we try to justify our sinful ways, we fall victim to the lie of our imagination. Over time, those lies enslave our hearts and minds if we do not dethrone them. And in a culture where actions play out in real-time and on the big screen, we don't have the luxury of ignoring minor indiscretions. Lies lead to self-deception, and deception leads to death. If we have aspirations of making it to the next level, we have to clean out the sinful things concealed within our closets. Our prayer should be for discernment to know and see the things that threaten our influence.

I want to wrap up this chapter by hearkening back to the story of Adam and Eve. As I shared earlier, their sideswipe with sin left them physically and emotionally uncovered. When God confronted the first couple about their sins, they blamed each other and then blamed an enemy. When the truth came out, they were both found guilty. Neither Adam nor Eve followed God's commands, and they knowingly disobeyed his instructions. Their feeble attempt to use fig leaves as a covering proved insufficient.

Perhaps God views anything that man uses to hide his spiritual shame as cursed, and maybe that's why Jesus stopped to place a curse on a fig tree when he walked the earth. I don't think it is a stretch of the imagination to connect the two events.

Today, we wouldn't dare think of using fig leaves. Instead, we try to cloak our identities in fame, influence, careers, philanthropic gestures, or any other thing that would attempt to distance our authenticity. Whatever that covering is, it cannot bear fruit and is doomed to wither away. Maybe you are in a similar situation, away from God and hiding behind your actions. We've all been there.

The good news is that we can reclaim our credibility by owning up to our mistakes and taking accountability for our conduct. It's time we step out of the shadows and into significance. Like Adam and Eve, we must own up to our indiscretions and pay attention to the minor infractions that would steal away our futures. It's also time for us to step into the presence of God and let the shallowness of our insecurities fall to the ground.

4

Love Yourself

Olivia was adamant about not having her senior picture taken. From the time she was an early teen, Olivia had suffered from outbreaks of severe acne. The skin disorder had left deep scars on her face, making her intensely self-conscious. She avoided group photos, and individual photos were out of the question. Olivia's mother tried to reason, "But they can use a photo editing app to remove the scars." Olivia softened at this possibility and moved forward with having her picture taken. When the photos arrived, she was reluctant to look at them, but once she did, she was happy to see that all traces of her acne were removed from the image. With a smile, she said, "Now that is the real me!"

Most people would likely change something about their appearance if given the opportunity. Without a doubt, we would alter the perception that people have of us. The truth of it was that when Olivia looked at the touched-up picture of herself, she didn't realize that it didn't truly represent what she looked like. It was a modified image of how she wanted others to perceive her.

When you look in the mirror, who do you see staring back? Do you see the same person who other people see? Do you stare at a person who others *want* you to be? Or do you see the person who you long to be? The other day I was reading a Scripture passage that tied in perfectly with this thought. In Paul's letter to the church at Corinth, he used a similar metaphor to help them understand that we skew our self-perception when we single out our imperfections:

> We see things imperfectly, like puzzling reflec-
> tions in a mirror, but then we will see every-
> thing with perfect clarity. All that I know now
> is partial and incomplete, but then I will know
> everything completely, just as God now knows
> me completely. (1 Corinthians 13:12 NLT)

I can't help but think of carnivals and fun houses that hold dozens of mirrors that distort your reflection. I recall one mirror that made me look taller than my actual size, another made me look a foot shorter, while other mirrors twisted and contorted my shape altogether. Thankfully, the last mirror gave an honest reflection of my proportions. When it comes to self-image, we must be sure that the mirror we are using is accurate and not warped. This idea is what lingered in James' mind when he wrote: "If you listen to the word and don't obey, it is like glancing at your face in a mirror. You see yourself, walk away, and forget what you look like" (James 1:23–24 NLT).

The Word of God is the benchmark of truth. When we dive deep into his truths, we cannot help but see the authentic version of ourselves. Over the years, I have watched leaders lose the image of who they aspired to be, letting it slip through the cracks and waste away. They lose the passion that once drove them to success. It would be hard for me to count the number of promising young men and women who let their own authenticity creep right out of their lives. When we forget that our authenticity is the driving point of our careers, we need to trace our journey back to the beginning and discover what changed the nature of our character. We need to look around and see if we've developed blind spots. Blind spots can be anything that obstructs our view of the truth. Sometimes those blind spots are found within our character, and trust me when I say that these kinds of issues don't fade away simply because we ignore them.

We all have shortcomings and weaknesses, and sometimes we need an honest friend to point them out. And if we repeatedly hear the same observation from different people, there is probably some truth to it. Permitting others to speak freely about realities that may cause personal offense can even be our saving grace because positive transformation occurs when we have conversations about things we would just as soon avoid. I have found that solid leaders embrace words of caution. So when someone is kind enough to throw out caution flags for us, we should be mature enough to yield to their warning and be grateful for it.

When I think of a strong leader who almost missed a great opportunity, my mind draws up the image of Naaman. As a famous Syrian general, Naaman was honored by the king for his long list of victories. The reputation he had chiseled out was that of a heroic warrior. But he had a dreadful secret: Naaman had leprosy. And he needed more than medical assistance; he needed a miracle.

Just when Naaman felt there was no hope for his condition, his life took a bizarre twist. One day, a servant girl told Naaman's wife a wide-eyed tale about a prophet who could heal Naaman's disease. Filled with hope, the Syrian king sent Naaman to the neighboring king of Israel and asked for a connection with the prophet. After the exchange of a few letters, the prophet Elisha agreed to see Naaman. However, when Naaman arrived at the meeting place, Elisha refused to meet with him in person. Instead, he sent word through one of the servants that if Naaman wanted to recover, he would have to go and bathe in the Jordan River. The story gets even more bizarre when the prophet adds on to that order that Naaman would have to repeat the ceremonial washing seven times.

You can probably imagine that the instruction landed hollow in the head of Naaman. Angry, Naaman stormed away shouting:

> "I thought he would certainly come out to
> meet me!" he said. "I expected him to wave
> his hand over the leprosy and call on the name
> of the LORD his God and heal me! Aren't

the rivers of Damascus, the Abana, and the
Pharpar better than any of the rivers of Israel?
Why shouldn't I wash in them and be healed?"
So Naaman turned and went away in a rage.
But his officers tried to reason with him and
said, "Sir, if the prophet had told you to do
something very difficult, wouldn't you have
done it? So you should certainly obey him
when he says simply, 'Go and wash and be
cured!'" So Naaman went down to the Jordan
River and dipped himself seven times, as the
man of God had instructed. And his skin
became as healthy as the skin of a young child,
and he was healed! (2 Kings 5:10–14 NLT)

I have often wondered why Naaman was so angry. I imagine that the source of his rage was rooted in the fact that the
prophet did not honor Naaman's position as a man who had
accomplished great military exploits. To be dismissed without
the courtesy of a formal greeting was probably humiliating compared to the fanfare Naaman customarily received. I also imagine that Naaman had a preconceived idea of how God was going
to heal him.

According to Scripture, Naaman expected that the prophet
would at least wave his hand dramatically over the leprosy or say
some commanding words that would initiate the healing. But to
order him to wash in the Jordan River seemed beneath Naaman's
dignity. After all, they had lavish healing pools in Syria; why not

send him there? The instruction to wash in the dirty waters of the Jordan flipped an emotional trigger, and Naaman went from being agitated to full throttle rage.

Anger clouded his ability to reason. And an outburst of rage almost cost him an opportunity to receive healing. Thankfully, Naaman had confidants who offered him a healthy dose of humility. Approaching Naaman in humility and deference, a servant offered him some advice, "My father, if the prophet had told you to do something great, would you not have done it?" (v. 13 NKJV). It was a cautious way of implying that if the prophet had asked him to do something that would have fed his ego, he would have quickly responded. But the last thing Naaman wanted was to be brought down in front of his men. In his heart, he probably thought, *I may be a leper, but I'm not letting go of this pride.*

The servant who approached Naaman continued to push past Naaman's arrogance and tried to sew together some logic. More or less, he told him that the prophet did not deny him healing but that healing would occur if he washed in the Jordan. It's almost as if he said, "Do you want to be healed or not?" Desperate, Naaman weighed his options and reluctantly trudged back to the Jordan River.

Let's pause for a moment and revisit some crucial facts about the story. This tale opens with a servant girl suggesting that Naaman seek out a prophet. The prophet then directs Naaman to the Jordan River. And finally, a man under Naaman's command convinces him to journey back and follow the prophet's instructions. At each stage of the story, Naaman must rely on the wisdom of those around him. He needed others to think and respond in a way that did not make sense to him at the time. Just like Naaman, there will be moments in our lives when we will need the wisdom, guidance, and faith of those who can see clearly during our darkest moments.

Maybe it's just my imagination, but I would assume that Naaman would not have worn his garments in the muddy Jordan River. If he were like most men, he would strip bare and wade right on in. Even though Naaman was a general, he would have worn clothes that would have identified him as a leper. Removing the worn-out rags that represented his condition was a subtle act of surrender. It was an outward sign that he was willing to be transparent in front of his men. It was also the first step in allowing healing to transpire. When his clothes fell to the ground, so did his pride. As he stood bare, his trusted soldiers saw the full measure of Naaman's condition. I am confident those leprosy sores were repulsive to see. It took a lot of guts for Naaman to reveal his covered-up sores. Just like Naaman, if we want to live and lead in an emotionally healthy way, then we must push through pride and let others see our true condition.

The miraculous part of the story happened next. After dipping seven times in the Jordan, Naaman's restored flesh was like that of a child. Because he was willing to follow an illogical instruction, Naaman was no longer a leader plagued with leprosy. He was a leader who found grace to defeat the issue that had been dominating him. He went from being a leader controlled by hidden problems to being a leader who confronted and conquered his issues—no more shame—no more distancing himself from people—no more fear of a shortened career. No more being labeled a leper. That one act of obedience shifted his entire identity. He was free to be a warrior without any undue burdens.

Like Naaman, most leaders have issues they need to confront. Even if they think they've quietly tucked them away, those who know them best are fully aware or at least suspicious of the problems that lie beneath the surface. It is when we humble ourselves before God and God's chosen authority over us that we will experience a change in our identity. The simple act of holding ourselves accountable is proof that we are serious about safeguarding our identity. I appreciate Dr. Myles Monroe's perspective on identity: "If you are still looking for that one person that can change your life, look in the mirror."

Consider that the first step to building a sidewalk is to form the exterior frame. Once the frame is securely in place, we fill the forms with concrete. We remove the wooden frames after the concrete cures, and the shape is permanent. In much the same way, leaders are formed. The frame is the structure or outline of who they want to become. The concrete represents one's resolve to mold into the image of who they aspire to become. Over time character fills in the frame and becomes a firm mold that can stand without the assistance of external props. In each of our lives, it takes time to establish healthy leadership habits that will empower us to be influential leaders.

Take influential leader John Lennon for example. Before he was a famous musician, he wrote poetry and sketched. At one point, he discovered that his Aunt Mimi had thrown away much of his art: "I used to say, 'Don't you destroy my papers.' I'd come home when I was fourteen and she (Aunt Mimi) had rooted all my things and thrown all my poetry out. I was saying, 'One day I'll be famous and you're going to regret it.'"[13] In his mind, he believed he would evolve into a famous entertainer. He took that mental impression and worked hard at cultivating that image. He succeeded, and his music influenced an entire generation and the generations to come.

The Bible makes it clear that our identities are securely anchored in what our hearts believe to be true. King Solomon wrote, "For as he thinks in his heart, so is he" (Proverbs 23:7 NKJV). He succinctly described the link between our identity and our self-image. If we were to list our attributes, what characteristics would we place on that list? Would we be objective enough to accurately put down our strengths and weaknesses? When we look into the mirror of our hearts, we may not like the person staring back at us. More often than not, we react to our damaged image with a lack of self-confidence, or our opinion of ourselves is warped by comparing our gifts and talents to others. What image of success have you created within your mind? Do you see yourself in a way that moves you toward your goals?

Research shows that people's words and opinions shape how we see ourselves. In many ways, the people we surround ourselves with directly reflect how we see ourselves. In her study, "Power of Teachers' Words: The Influence on Pupils' Grades and Behaviour," Magdalena Podobińska learned that students who were spoken over negatively and then issued a mock test scored low. The same students given a mock test after being spoken over affirmatively scored significantly higher.[14] Without a doubt, there is a strong correlation between affirmation and actions. Words have the power to shape our self-image in ways we cannot even imagine. As leaders or mentors, our words shape the future for those who follow us. Our responsibility is to draw out the gifts, talents, and characters of those following in our footsteps.

When I think of fathers and how they shape the lives of their sons, I'm reminded of the biblical account of Isaac. From the moment Jacob caught his twin brother's heel coming out of the womb, Isaac labeled his son as one who would be a "supplanter; one who grasps, trips up, or deceives."[15] Whether he knew the significance of this decision or not, Isaac was prophesying Jacob's future. Before long, Jacob began to act on those words. Jewish history reminds us he was the one who cheated his brother out of his birthright (Genesis 25:27–34). Isaac's words shaped the future of his son. The definition of his name became a prophetic prediction over Jacob's future. Whether we like it or not, we tend to give great attention to the words ascribed to us by our parents and mentors.

One of the underlying goals of Zig Ziglar's book *See You at the Top* was to help individuals increase their self-confidence. Another popular book, *The Power of Positive Thinking* by Norman Vincent Peale, helped readers grasp a positive self-portrait and embrace the idea they could achieve anything with God's help. These books inspired many to believe in themselves, and as a result, they became successful leaders and entrepreneurs.

How we see ourselves determines what goals we are willing to reach. Consider how the Israelites wandered through the wilderness and had front row tickets to majestic miracles, then days later, they let their faith evaporate into thin air. When it was time to see the promised fulfillment, they allowed self-doubt to rob them of the inheritance. We find this long and winding journey in the book of Numbers, but for now, I will pull out and highlight a few pieces of this tale.

As the Israelites neared the promised land, Moses, their leader, sent twelve men to spy out the land. When they returned from their under-cover mission, the report they gave seemed like something spun out of a fairy tale. They described honeycombs that were the size of humans and grapes so grand they had to be carted around by men on poles. These weren't made-up images from men who needed to spin a good story. These were facts, and they brought back samples as proof.

One would think their discovery would have encouraged the band of followers, but it yielded the opposite effect. Moses was shocked at the men's reaction to their good fortune. Those who had seen the land firsthand said, "We are not able to go up against the people, for they are stronger than we" (Numbers 13:31 NKJV). And they gave the children of Israel an unfavorable report of the land which they had spied out, saying, "The land through which we have gone as spies is a land that devours its inhabitants, and all the people whom we saw in it are men of great stature. There we saw the giants...and we were like grasshoppers in our own sight, and so we were in their sight" (vv. 32–33). The simple act of self-comparison instilled doubt and fear in their hearts and nailed shut their resolve to pursue the riches of the land in front of them.

I know many who believe in the awesomeness of God but get tangled up when it comes to recognizing the greatness God has placed within them. The truth is we will never grow beyond our internal self-confidence, nor will we outperform the picture we have in our minds of our identity. The shepherd boy David was able to topple a giant twice his size because he saw himself as a victor and not a victim (1 Samuel 17). If we were to rewind the script of David's life, we would find his story didn't begin when he faced off with Goliath. His legacy's soft launch started when the prophet Samuel showed up at his house searching for the future king.

God sent Samuel to Jesse's house to anoint one of Jesse's eight sons to be the successor to the throne after King Saul. What makes this story memorable is that each one of Jesse's sons looked like he had the potential to fill the role of royalty. After inspecting seven of his sons, God reveals to Samuel that the chosen one was not in this group. Although they looked qualified, none of these men possessed the heart or passion God was looking for in a leader.

Samuel asked Jesse if he had any other sons. Jesse nodded and called for his youngest son David, who was out taking care of sheep. God knew what others had overlooked, that David had the heart of a warrior and the compassion of a shepherd. The new king God was looking for was David, the person to whom all the world would fall at his feet (1 Samuel 13). David did not gain his fame by having a handful of surface-level followers. David led from the heart. His leadership spilled over into the lives of those who followed in his footsteps. Their allegiance to David would shape them into warriors who would kill giants of their own.

God sees within each of us gifts, talents, and callings that others might overlook. When God looks at our future, he does not focus on our faults and failures; he peels back the layers and, through the loving lens of his grace, sees our potential. God sees us in his image and likeness. He sees us as his children living freely in his love. If we can see past our failures, then we can open up and love ourselves authentically. It's been my observation over the years that leaders who love themselves have a greater capacity to love their followers, and leaders who love their followers gain loyalty and allegiance.

Ultimately, it is time spent in the presence of God that brings about the most significant transformation of our hearts. He stands ready to strip away any falsehood that we have embraced about ourselves and is prepared to cloak us with confidence and courage. He longs to show us our undiscovered uniqueness and celebrate our individuality. Paul says it best, "We all, with unveiled face, beholding as in a mirror the glory of the Lord, are being transformed into the same image from glory to glory, just as by the Spirit of the Lord" (2 Corinthians 3:18 NKJV).

5

Embrace Authenticity

Chris always wanted a Rolex watch, but given the cost, he knew it far exceeded his price point. While on a work-related trip to Taiwan, he stumbled upon a small storefront displaying various Rolex watches. The owner saw him staring through the window and invited him inside to take a closer look. The prices were a dead giveaway that they were not genuine Rolex watches, but they were priced in a range he could afford, and they looked almost identical to the real brand.

He thought to himself, *Who will know whether or not my watch is a knockoff?* He made the purchase without a second thought and slid the watch onto his wrist. Over the next few weeks, he received several compliments on it, but the compliments would quickly turn to laughter when the truth of its origin came to light.

One night, while attending a company dinner for upper management, the unthinkable happened. Chris, dressed in formal attire and seated at the head table, noticed that his watchband had loosened and slid down his wrist, revealing an odd greenish stain that wrapped around his arm. The artificial, gold-plated band exposed the truth of the watch's authenticity (or lack thereof). The desire to impress his peers had backfired, and the once-prized watch found its way into the trash bin. Just because a thing shares a semblance to something of value does not mean that it also shares its worth. Chris's wristwatch had the Rolex name inscribed on the forgery's face, but in no way did it represent the quality of a true Rolex wristwatch.

If you have studied art or visited an art museum, then you may already be aware that pieces of fine art are often forged and sold at outrageous prices as if they were original masterpieces. After undergoing renovations, a small, state-owned museum in Elne, France, held a grand reopening that featured the paintings of local artist Étienne Terrus, a contemporary of Henri Matisse. As fate would have it, an art expert with a keen eye noticed something strange about a particular Terrus canvas. Upon closer inspection, the art expert identified an irregularity: One of the buildings appearing in the painting had not been constructed until years after the artist had died, which meant that the painting hanging in the French museum was a forgery. Upon further investigation, experts discovered that eighty-two of the 140 works on display in the museum were not painted by Terrus at all. Art lovers felt betrayed and victimized by the scam artist, and the museum's reopening ended in scandal.[16]

Pieces of fine art and high-end collectibles are not the only things people scrutinize for authenticity. Those we lead often want to know if we as leaders truly are who we claim to be. They may not ask us directly; instead, they look for signature marks and hallmark signs that distinguish the real from the fake. Or they may seek information by scrolling through our social media timelines, talking to our closest friends, and scrutinizing our behavior. This is why leaders must become comfortable living under scrutiny.

Numerous biblical leaders faced enormous pressure to appease the people who followed them. One early example is Moses. In every season of leadership, the Israelites placed pressure on Moses to perform God's work on their terms. Before we get too far ahead of the story, let's stop and consider Moses' résumé. For forty years, he was a shepherd. Then he contended with Pharaoh to free the enslaved Israelites. He facilitated ten mesmerizing miracles. He led a nation out of captivity and, by faith, believed that God would part the Red Sea. And this was all within the first half of this man's life. If you read the book of Exodus, you can trace the ways God confirmed Moses' leadership. Every crisis has a pivotal point, and through Moses God guided his people to success.

In one sticky situation, God sent an angel ahead of Moses to ensure victory (Exodus 23:20). By etching his commands on tablets of stone, God established Moses as governor over his people (Exodus 20). At the command of Moses, miracles flowed into and over the people who stuck close to his lead. And if you only read about the supernatural miracles that happened, then you would assume that Moses secured a hundred percent approval rating from his followers. But as is the case with all good leaders, some followers will always think you should have done more or done things differently. Moses' crowd was no different; the people challenged every decision he made: where he led them, what they ate, and what he wore. Even his family members felt bold enough to question whom Moses chose to marry.

For the life of me, I cannot imagine the pressure he felt even without the peering eyes of social media followers. I know of far too many leaders who walk away from their futures because of the pressure from uncaring people. Solid leaders, on the other hand, develop the confidence to lead from the offense, not the defense. And over time, their success speaks louder than their critics. One thing I admire about Moses is how he let the miracles do the talking. It's hard to face off with someone who can verbally command the earth to part and swallow up his or her opposition. Before we leave off talking about Moses's life, I do want to highlight one passage that revealed what happened when an inner-circle group created a coup against God's leaders:

> They rose up before Moses, with a number of the people of Israel, 250 chiefs of the congregation, chosen from the assembly, well-known men. They assembled themselves together against Moses and against Aaron and said to them, "You have gone too far! For all in the

congregation are holy, every one of them, and
the Lord is among them. Why then do you
exalt yourselves above the assembly of the
Lord?" When Moses heard it, he fell on his
face, and he said to Korah and all his company,
"In the morning the Lord will show who is his,
and who is holy, and will bring him near to
him. The one whom he chooses he will bring
near to him." (Numbers 16:2–5 ESV)

The best way to summarize this story is to say that God
grew weary of hearing his best man criticized. In this situation,
God decided the best way to shut down the censorship was to
bury the faultfinders alive. I'm not sure that Moses expected that
kind of response, but sometimes God cares for his elect in ways
deemed unpopular by the public.

We could analyze history books and study great philos-
ophers, but the most outstanding, successful leader to ever live
was Jesus Christ. The religious and political leaders of Jesus' time
felt threatened by his popularity. Paradoxically, he used simple
parables to teach the principles of the kingdom of God, and his
wisdom confounded rabbis.

Jesus' teachings were not the only thing that came under
fire. The miracles he performed also incited irritation and anger
in those who could or would not accept that his source of power
was not of this world. In the midst of every miracle were those
who called into question the validity or authenticity of his

authority. When Jesus cast demons out of a man, they accused him of cooperating with the father of demons (Matthew 9:32–34). Considering the countless number of witnesses from countless miracles, one would think that those of his generation would embrace him as the Son of God. The truth of the old adage is wrong: Seeing is *not always* believing.

Throughout all three years of Jesus' earthly ministry, critics questioned his identity. They demanded demonstrations and signs to prove his divinity. When the pressure was on, Jesus refused to yield to the demands of the crowd. He gave them space to speculate and consider, but he never succumbed to the pressure to perform. In a not-so-subtle way, Jesus told them they would receive the sign of Jonah (Matthew 12:39). It was a cryptic reference to his death and resurrection that many would not understand until years later.

Numerous leaders overloaded with stress have admitted to me that the pressure has left them questioning their purpose and their ability to lead others effectively. I am sure that you've experienced moments in your life that left you second-guessing your identity and self-worth. We all have. And I am often quick to remind leaders that even Jesus withdrew from the noise and gave great thought to the road that lay before him. While alone in the garden of Gethsemane, he had to come to terms with the fact that the cross stood between him and a crown. Jesus faced his fate at that moment.

Knowing he would die an excruciating death, Jesus asked for an alternative to the horror of dying naked on a cross. And there beneath an olive tree, Jesus asked his Father if it was possible to avoid drinking the cup of God's judgment for sin. He felt the oppressive weight of the hour and said to his disciples, "My soul is crushed with grief to the point of death. Stay here and keep watch with me" (Mark 14:34 NLT). The heavy feeling that came with knowing his life was the price for humanity's redemption was so intense that his sweat turned into blood.

Pressure is often the litmus test of character for leaders, and the quality of our leadership subsequently surfaces. Stress pulls out of us either courage or cowardliness. It magnifies our strengths and weaknesses. Those crucial moments lead us to victory or failure of our assignment. In the case of Jesus, the cross was the path to the kingdom. He understood that submitting to divine authority was the key to possessing earthly authority, and because he humbled himself and became a servant, Jesus obtained all power and authority (Philippians 2: 8–11).

Leaders need to understand that subjecting to authority is by far more of an asset than a liability. In fact, one of the greatest secrets to growing as a leader is to submit to wiser, more experienced leaders. When we are willing to do that, we signal to the world that we are humble, obedient, and teachable.

If we were to revisit the garden of Gethsemane one more time, we would see that when the soldiers came to arrest Jesus, they asked him to verify his identity; they would not arrest him without confirmation that he was the one the crowds called "miracle maker." And when Jesus confirmed that he was who they were looking for, using the words *I am* to confirm his identity, the soldiers fell backward at the mention of his name (John 18:6). He referenced the name that God used to identify himself to Moses at the burning bush (Exodus 3:14). After such a display of power, one would suppose that they would have feared to take him into custody, and maybe they did. But greater than their fear of Jesus' identity was their fear of religious and political forces.

Even while he was nailed to the cross, the crowd heckled him over his identity, "If you are the King of the Jews, save yourself!" (Luke 23:37 ESV). "If you are the Son of God, come down from the cross" (Matthew 27:40 ESV). It would have been easy for Jesus to blink himself off the cross and crucify his critics instead. But that is not the kind of leadership Jesus wanted to model. His goal was redemption not retaliation. His eyes were glued to the Father, not the faultfinders.

One of the things that drew people to Jesus was his resolve to stay true to the identity that the Father had given him. Three times God spoke from heaven and declared Jesus as his Son (Matthew 3:17; Matthew 17:5; Hebrews 5:5). Jesus confirmed this identity by holding fast to characteristics that emulated his heavenly Father. Just as we recognize that character traits can pass from parent to child, so, too, did Jesus exemplify distinctive godly virtues. His actions, words, and deeds reflected God. The words his Father spoke were the words Jesus spoke. The works he saw his Father do were the works he performed. Not one critic managed to pressure Jesus into denying the identity his Father gave him.

One of the unique details of John's account of the crucifixion was the sign that hung above Jesus' head. Carved in Hebrew, Greek, and Latin was the title, "Jesus of Nazareth, King of the Jews." It was humanity's effort to challenge Jesus' identity one last time. In a passive way, it mocked him. Still Jesus denied himself the privilege of justice and focused on the reward of completing his calling. In a way that few master, he became a suffering sacrifice for the greater good of those he loved.

On more occasions than I feel comfortable revealing, I've met leaders who were driven to earn titles and public recognition. They pursue these hollow things in an effort to affirm their own value when it should be a reflection of responsibility. Titles describe accomplishments, but they do not define character. Leaders should focus on demonstrating humility and dignity regardless of whether they obtain public recognition. I am mindful that giftedness and experience may place us in positions of leadership, but character determines our position of influence. The humility Jesus displayed on the cross reflected his character and not the carefully crafted title displayed above his head. Read this passage and imagine the emotions and feelings Jesus experienced:

> He was despised and rejected by men, a man
> of sorrows and acquainted with grief; and as
> one from whom men hide their faces, he was
> despised, and we esteemed him not. Surely, he
> has borne our griefs and carried our sorrows;
> yet we esteemed him stricken, smitten by God,
> and afflicted. But he was pierced for our trans-
> gressions; he was crushed for our iniquities;
> upon him was the chastisement that brought
> us peace, and with his wounds we are healed.
> (Isaiah 53:3–5 ESV)

It's impossible for us to wrap our minds around the physical suffering Jesus experienced on the cross. Without going into great detail, his suffering included a crown of thorns, being spit upon and slapped, having his beard plucked from his face, and receiving at least thirty-nine stripes on his body from straps filled with bone and metal fragments. As the hour of horror unraveled, Jesus looked toward heaven and whispered the words, "Father, forgive them" (Luke 22:34 ESV). In a moment of unimaginable pain, what was in his heart found its way out of his mouth. His love for humanity came down to three simple words. He endured the cross because he set his eyes on the reward that would come from saving God's sons and daughters. As leaders, we must intentionally maintain our focus during tumultuous times.

If we circle back to the crucifixion and pay attention to the details, we notice that soldiers gambled for Jesus' garments. In a final gesture to rob him of any dignity, they stripped Jesus bare and wagered over his wardrobe. It sounds insignificant unless we connect it to Adam, the first man God created, and yet Scripture calls Jesus "the last Adam" (1 Corinthians 15:45).

When the first Adam sinned, he hid among the trees with Eve. And when they crept out to present their guilt, in true divine fashion, God demonstrated his grace. He covered them with coats made from cloth. To be more specific, he cloaked them in skins taken from slain animals. I know that sounds graphic, but it was a message to humankind that it would require a blood sacrifice for humanity to stand in God's presence. The first Adam brought sin and death into the world.

The last Adam, Jesus, substituted sin for eternal life. Metaphorically, God took fig leaves from Adam and garments from Jesus. It was a slight detail, but God included it within humanity's history. It was not only an image but also a reminder that Jesus was unclothed so that his righteousness could clothe us. He sacrificed himself to save us.

Sacrifice comes with leadership. Think of Captain Edward Smith of the Titanic, known as an unsinkable ship and a modern marvel. It stunned the world when it sank on its maiden voyage. More heartbreaking was the fifteen hundred people who died in the icy waters of the North Atlantic. Only 705 survived. History revealed that Captain Smith went down with the ship, placing the lives of his crew and passengers above his own. That's genuine commitment to leadership: sacrificing one's well-being for the security of others.

Leadership also demands the resolve to develop those in your charge, and confident leaders do this intentionally. Truthfully, I've not met many effective leaders who were threatened by the success of those they trained. Most are passionate and excited to see their followers become successful, often more so than themselves. The more that we as leaders invest in the lives of our followers, the more secure our relationships with them become. Before long, followers take on a family-like familiarity. Jesus did this perfectly. He took a ragtag group of men and invested three years in their personal development. He taught them, believed in them, prayed for them, empowered them, and released them to live out their destinies. It was out of their strong relationships with Jesus that all but one of his disciples died a martyr's death. They were willing to place their lives on the line because they understood the depth of his love for them.

One modern leader who worked hard to form stable relationships with his followers was former president and victorious general Dwight D. Eisenhower. I read an article by John Addison about this celebrated historical figure that helped me understand him as a unique leader. Addison identified five of Eisenhower's bold leadership qualities that we can seek to develop ourselves: be likeable, practice optimism, control your ego, know your purpose, and take responsibility.[17]

Be likeable. Being a likable leader is often an overlooked attribute that yields great rewards. Likeability builds morale, morale leads to enthusiasm, enthusiasm fosters confidence, and confidence creates success.

Practice optimism. Leaders who exude optimism attract enthusiastic followers. One of the greatest football coaches of all time is Lou Holtz. He trained his players to view life and football through the lens of optimism. Through a unique style of leadership, he elevated the potential of his players. He convinced them their destiny was to win. They lived out those expectations.

Control your ego. Few, if any, people will want to follow leaders who operate out of self-interest or believe themselves above reproach. Eisenhower "had a giant ego, as well as a huge temper he struggled to contain. But he knew when to stay quiet, to appear to acquiesce, while thinking how to gain advantage several moves ahead."[18]

Know your purpose. Successful leaders provide a vision or a purpose for others to carry out to the end. For Eisenhower, it was to train an army to win World War II. For Lou Holtz, it was to develop his players to win an NCAA championship.

Take responsibility. One thing both Eisenhower and Holtz shared was a refusal to transfer failure to others. As leaders, whether they won or lost, they took responsibility for those under their charge. President Harry Truman said it best: "The buck stops here." When a leader takes responsibility, he or she wins over the heart of those following.

These qualities remind me of a learning experience from my own life. With great excitement and enthusiasm, my wife and I served a small fledgling church on the edge of town. It was our first pastorate, and we worked hard to help the church grow. Before long, our congregation had expanded to the point that we needed a larger building. During this same time, another minister felt compelled to start a new church just miles from our location. After some discussion, a meeting was called for pastors to discuss a new church's viability in the area. At the meeting, the new minister presented his vision and followed up with questions and answers. A few pastors spoke up and openly expressed their opinions. But one comment shook me to the core. In a heartless reference to our church, the denomination overseer for our state said that my church had never grown and probably never would. My heart sank. I felt like the world's greatest failure, and that one opinion nearly crushed my vision.

A few days later, I attended a large gathering in which the state overseer was present. As I walked up the auditorium steps, he motioned for me to walk his way. I braced myself and thought, *More criticism to come.* As I neared, we exchanged greetings, and

I attempted to hide my feelings. The words that tumbled out of his mouth surprised me: "Son, I was irritated by one of the comments in the meeting we had earlier this week, and I misspoke. I did not mean what I said. You are one of our outstanding young pastors. I would never want to speak a word that hurt one of our ministers. Please, forgive me." And I did.

From that moment forward, whenever I saw him, he went out of his way to speak an encouraging word to me. A man whom I honored had hurt me. However, when he apologized, I saw the heart of a true leader. My trust in him grew overnight because he took responsibility for his actions. When he humbled himself, he proved his love for me. His humility did not cause me to think less of him but more. He was who he said he was: my leader.

When our authenticity is tried, it brings forth evidence that speaks for itself. God does not test us to discover what's within us; he already knows. We have nothing to prove. Instead, he tests us so that we discover it for ourselves. We are who we are by the grace of God.

6

Overcome Failure

R*ocky* is one of the most successful movies of all time. The film's central character is Rocky Balboa, a slugging, unpolished prizefighter. The movie's star, Sylvester Stallone, continued the story in sequels to allow fans to follow the life of this fictitious boxer. Having an inner desire to be the champion, Rocky refuses to quit. Sometimes he wins; other times he loses, but in almost every movie, Rocky suffers a beating. Something about his character resonates with so many people, and something about the movie's theme song, "Eye of the Tiger," stirs us to pull ourselves up from the mat of defeat and strive for the win. We all want to be the champ, the winner, and winning means being the last person standing.

Losing does not come easy to a natural-born leader. If caught off guard, the anguish that comes with feeling inferior can invite feelings of insecurity and self-doubt. Even leaders who are usually confident and carefree can find themselves suffering from the sudden shock of unexpected failure. It is usually during those times that issues of the heart find their way to the surface for all to see.

As I scan through the Bible and study various leaders, my thoughts often land on the apostle Simon Peter. His actions and reactions are textbook examples of what happens when leaders make impulsive, thoughtless decisions. One night, before the crucifixion, Jesus talked to his apostles about their forthcoming failures. In a candid way, he gave them a two-fold prophecy: They would fail, and he would pray for them to recover from failure. In a roundabout way, he explained that failure doesn't negate favor. Through prayer and a repentant heart, today's mistakes can be the launch pad for tomorrow's miracles. That truth found its way to the apostle Simon Peter:

> "Simon, listen! Satan has demanded to have you apostles for himself. He wants to separate you from me as a farmer separates wheat from husks. But I have prayed for you, Simon, that your faith will not fail. So when you recover, strengthen the other disciples."
>
> But Peter said to him, "Lord, I'm ready to go to prison with you and to die with you."

Jesus replied, "Peter, I can guarantee that the rooster won't crow tonight until you say three times that you don't know me." (Luke 22:31–34 GW)

Simon (Peter) convinced himself that he was prepared to die for Jesus, but he wasn't. The words of Jesus' prophecy shortly came to pass in the garden of Gethsemane. Judas, another disciple, led a midnight mob to where Jesus was praying. In a sinister scuffle, Peter drew his sword and took a swipe at a guard's head, severing his ear. In a way that only grace can respond, Jesus reached out and reattached the guard's ear.

After the chief priests arrested Jesus, Peter followed behind from a safe distance. While Jesus was under interrogation by the council of scribes and elders, Peter cowered in the courtyard. As Jesus had warned, Peter was not yet a strong enough leader to stand up for the truth. When bystanders asked him about his relationship to Jesus, Peter swore, "I do not know the man" (Matthew 26:72). Not once, not twice, but three times Peter had a chance to die with Jesus, as he had promised. And three times he failed.

Peter wasn't the only one who went against their word that night. The Scriptures say that all the other disciples fled the scene (Matthew 26:56). After everyone cleared out, there was another odd twist to the story: "All the disciples abandoned him and ran away. A certain young man was following Jesus. He had nothing on but a linen sheet. They tried to arrest him, but he left the linen sheet behind and ran away naked" (Mark 14:50–52 GW).

Mark, the author of this passage, added this detail, while the other gospel writers missed or omitted it. Or perhaps that detail was inserted for personal reasons. Regardless, if you tracked Mark's history, you would find that whenever life got complicated, Mark would cut and run. That kind of behavior happened on more than one occasion and cost him an internship and a high-profile opportunity. While on a missionary journey with Paul and Barnabas, Mark inexplicably deserted them and headed for home. This action created friction between Paul and Barnabas as to whether Mark should accompany them on their next assignment. They ultimately decided to part ways; Barnabas took Mark, and Paul took another associate named Silas (Acts 15: 36–41).

Every leader at one point or another has felt the tension between wanting to leave a difficult, messy situation or committing to stick it out to the end. If you are in that season of life, it may bring comfort to remember that even the hearts of giant killers like David pounded away during seasons of extreme pressure. In a frightening season, David wrote these words: "My heart pounds in my chest. The terror of death assaults me. Fear and trembling overwhelm me, and I can't stop shaking. Oh, that I had wings like a dove; then I would fly away and rest!" (Psalm 55:4–6 NLT).

I want to pause for a moment and share with you the remarkable, true story of Amber Williams, a friend of mine whose courage and determination to persevere inspires me. Born with cerebral palsy, her childhood was one of frustration and hardship. The constant barrage of verbal and physical abuse from classmates made her question whether life was worth living. She battled suicidal thoughts, depression, and the urge to run away to a different life. But she consciously decided to have a meaningful, blessed life. Against all odds, she graduated high school, married, and became the mother of two children. She contributed to her community by teaching a Sunday School class and eventually obtained full-time employment working with the homeless. Refusing to quit or run away from life, she persevered and reached her goals.

Even though it is tempting to run from overwhelming situations, the truth is that those situations tend to follow us wherever we may go to try to hide. When we are in dark seasons and feel like fleeing, one of the best things we can do is reach out to a mentor who will fight for our future. Going back to Rocky, he had a trainer who stayed the course and remained in Rocky's corner, cheering him on whenever he wanted to quit.

Although there are well-known leaders who stand out in the New Testament, a lesser-known leader played a critical role in moving the church forward. Barnabas was to the apostle Paul what Mickey was to Rocky. The name *Barnabas* means "encourager," and he lived up to that legacy. Since Paul was known for killing Christians, believers of that day had good reason to be skeptical of Paul when he wanted to become one himself. But Barnabas went against the tide of culture and was willing to gamble on how God might use Paul (Acts 9: 26–28). Barnabas gave Saul a chance when other leaders reached for stones. That's what leadership does: It takes risks on exiled, isolated individuals. And it is risk takers like Barnabas who cultivate courageous leaders like Paul. Maybe that is one reason Jesus encouraged us to "do to others as you would like them to do to you" (Luke 6:31 NLT). It is our responsibility to give out grace in the same measure that we wish to receive it.

Barnabas went on to influence other disciples, too, including John Mark. One interpretation breaks down the origin of John Mark's name to mean "grace" and "large hammer."[19] I know that sounds odd, but if you really think about the words, you will find that grace functions as a large hammer that shatters failure. Coming full circle while imprisoned and awaiting execution, Paul sends for Mark: "Only Luke is with me. Bring Mark with you when you come, for he will be helpful to me in my ministry" (2 Timothy 4:11 NLT). With the passage of time Mark went from being known as a deserter to becoming indispensable. With great fortitude, he rewrote how people would remember him and built back his credibility.

Most of us can relate to the idea that our ambitions sometimes ambush our potential. Take the 2002 Winter Olympics for example. Athletes from around the world were set to compete in the ice track 1000-meter race in Salt Lake City, Utah. In the final race, five skaters battled each other for the gold medal. Steven Bradbury, a skater from Australia, had qualified for the race by winning the bronze medal with the relay team at the 1994 games and was predicted to finish last. Knowing the odds, he devised a risky strategy that he hoped would give him an edge. As the senior skater of the bunch, he placed himself behind the younger, faster opponents. With each passing lap, it appeared Bradbury would finish last.

Then the unexpected happened. Li Jiajun from team China ambitiously attempted to pass the USA favorite Apolo Anton Ohno, who was in first place. The move Jiajun had practiced for four years went horribly wrong, and Ohno collided with the other skaters. Because he had been safely behind the leaders, Bradbury was the first to cruise over the finish line. Some believed Jiajun's overconfidence cost him the race. [20]

Public failure isn't just painful; it can prove catastrophic if experienced without hope for recovery. I know men and women who never regained their strength after slip-ups or scandals. The public scrutiny was a fatal stake driven deep into the heart of the leader. An excellent guideline on how to help a fellow leader recover from failure is found in a letter that St. Paul wrote to a small band of Christians: "If another believer is overcome by some sin…gently and humbly help that person back onto the right path. And be careful not to fall into the same temptation yourself" (Galatians 6:1 NLT).

I have learned from my own mistakes that there comes a point when we have to stop staring at our self-inflicted wounds and allow others to help bind them up. Although we may not feel like letting others reach out and help rescue us, that humility is a part of the healing process. Remember that pride resists the presence of others, but humility grabs hold of the hand that extends grace.

Not long ago I reached out to a friend who experienced a moral slip. It took months before he would even answer my call. Although he never explained why he was slow to respond, I knew it was because he felt embarrassed and unworthy of a friend. Later he admitted that his shame had convinced him that conversation with others would be too difficult; sitting alone in silence seemed his only salvation. We've all experienced seasons where solitude felt like our only solution. If you know of someone who has experienced the trauma of having stones thrown at them because of their behavior, don't let them sit and stare at their scars alone. Run to the wounded. Sometimes just pulling up a chair and sitting beside them can give them hope and help them see a way out of their situation.

To attack us when we are down is like pouring salt in a wound. Criticism does not permit healing to take place. Criticism is a seed that produces discouragement. It takes several compliments to undo one word of complaint. Zig Ziglar said, "Don't be distracted by criticism. Remember—the only taste of success some people have is when they take a bite out of you."[21]

If you have dealt with leaders, then you know that while most of them are not wired to receive pity, they can still be open to empathy. One of the best ways to comfort a leader is to speak hope concerning their future. In times of chaos, weigh out your words, making sure they are healing up wounds and not reopening them. Instead of focusing on the transgression, gently remind wounded colleagues of their worth. Point out times when they have made a difference in the business or in someone's life. Keep them focused on a future goal and remind them that God is still for them. Even after Peter denied Jesus, Jesus was gracious enough to remind him of his calling.

During seasons of failure, we need hope and positive reinforcement. Even Elon Musk, the young tech billionaire with an accrued net worth of more than $160 billion, has experienced his fair share of failure. His creativity includes innovations such as battery-powered cars, spaceships, and electronic inventions. Most people are unaware that he was fired from his position of CEO of his *Zip2* company. He also received news that he was ousted from PayPal while he was on his honeymoon. Following that, he led six failed SpaceX rocket launches, and both Tesla and SpaceX wavered on the brink of bankruptcy. When many would have given up their dreams, Musk continued to run toward his. Brilliant, creative, risk-taking, and a proven innovator, I can't help but wonder about the additional success he would have experienced if those companies would have believed in him.

It is easy for feelings of depression to creep in and rob our creativity. Whenever I am discouraged, I fall back on these verses:

> The Lord helps the fallen and lifts those bent beneath their loads. (Psalm 145:14 NLT)

> The Lord directs the steps of the godly. He delights in every detail of their lives. Though they stumble, they will never fall, for the Lord holds them by the hand. (Psalm 37:23–24 NLT)

For hope, I also like to turn to the book of Genesis and the tale of a young dreamer by the name of Joseph. The favorite son of his father, Jacob, Joseph was despised by his brothers. When Joseph was young, he made the mistake of sharing a series of prophetic dreams with his brothers, and those dreams predicted that his brothers would bow before him in a submissive posture.

Like any sibling rivalry, this created quite a stir. Filled with frustration over favoritism, the older brothers devised a scheme to drop Joseph into a deep well and then sell him to a band of slave traders. The drama went even darker when, to cover their deceptive tracks, they killed an animal and covered Joseph's clothing in blood to convince their father his favorite son was dead.

For years Jacob mourned the loss of Joseph. Then a famine hit the land. It wasn't the inflationary kind of scarcity but the kind that sent his brothers scrambling for scraps of food. On a quest for survival, they traveled to Egypt. In a way that only God could orchestrate, the brothers stumbled into the pharaoh's court, where Joseph was in charge of managing the nation's grain. What's interesting is that when Joseph's brothers stepped before him to request grain for their family, they had no idea who he was.

Time has an interesting way of propelling some individuals forward in a way that frustrates others. Although his brothers didn't recognize him, Joseph knew exactly who they were. Caught up in a whirlwind of emotions, he eventually let down his guard and revealed his identity. Offering a measure of grace that rivals any tale in history, he tearfully told them, "Don't be upset, and don't be angry with yourselves for selling me to this place. It was God who sent me here ahead of you to preserve your lives" (Genesis 45:5 NLT). His brothers then remembered the dreams Joseph had shared as a boy.

Aching to see his father, Joseph insisted that his brothers bring Jacob and the entire family to Egypt. When the brothers brought the truth to their father, Scripture spells out the scene this way:

"Joseph is still alive!" they told him. "And he is governor of all the land of Egypt!" Jacob was stunned at the news—he couldn't believe it. But when they repeated to Jacob everything Joseph had told them, and when he saw the wagons Joseph had sent to carry him, their father's spirits revived. Then Jacob exclaimed, "It must be true! My son Joseph is alive! I must go and see him before I die." (vv. 26–28 NLT)

When Jacob heard Joseph's story and saw the wagons of provision, he, too, remembered Joseph's dreams, and his spirit revived. Jacob went from mourner to worshiper. Joseph provided for his family to move to Egypt, and he gave them favorable portions in the land. Though Joseph had endured false accusations, imprisonment, and the rejection of his brothers, his dream remained alive. This story should give us hope that even when our dreams are delayed, they still have the potential to come to pass.

One key difference among those who succeed is their determination to get back up after a loss. Proverbs 24:16 says, "The righteous falls seven times and rises again" (ESV). David the great is another powerful example of how focusing on the future generates hope. In the sticky pages of his story, David and his men return home after the heat of the battle. They find their village pillaged and burned, and their wives and children are missing. Distraught and distressed, David's men consider stoning him: "David was greatly distressed, for the people spoke of stoning him because all the people were bitter in soul, each for his sons and daughters. But David strengthened himself in the LORD his God" (1 Samuel 30:6 ESV).

In this passage the word *strength* can be translated as "encouraged." Therefore, the text could read, "David *encouraged* himself in the LORD his God." When David stood in ashes that were once his village, he had no idea that he was three days away from recovering his losses and six days away from being anointed king of Judah. In moments of great distress, how do we talk to ourselves about our situation? Do we stumble around muttering like a madman, or do we recalibrate our thinking and focus on recovering? When I need to encourage myself, I pull from this Scripture passage, "Those who trust in the Lord will find new strength. They will soar high on wings like eagles. They will run and not grow weary. They will walk and not faint" (Isaiah 40:31 NLT).

Take a moment and think about the three levels of strength within that verse: power to soar above our problems and see things from a heavenly perspective; renew our strength to run with an abundance of energy; walk in the rhythm of newness. Whatever you need is found in the Lord. When others cannot help us, God will. As Green Bay Packers running back A.J. "The Sauce" Dillon posted on Twitter, "Whoever counted me out simply can't count!"[22]

7

Evaluate Relationships

Cheree' Haston, author of *When Leaders Fail* and *Sister Pastor*, recently said in a Facebook video teaching that "All leaders have secrets…They have trust issues…and if they don't feel like they can trust you, they will not be open and vulnerable." I wholeheartedly agree with her statement; we experience emotional pain when we trust the wrong person with our secrets. Singer and songwriter Dr. James Payne captured the same thought this way in a Twitter post: "Character assassination is usually brought by the hand of a trusted confidant."

It bothers me when I hear people say, "I trust people until they give me a reason not to." That kind of philosophy sounds good, but I've learned that this line of thinking so often leads to sorrow. When I was a teenager and started dating, my father routinely interrogated me with probing questions that made both of us uncomfortable. But he was willing to do so in order to hold me accountable for my actions. Like most teenagers, I accused him of not trusting me. And I wasn't prepared for his response: "Son, it isn't you I don't trust. I don't trust your flesh." His words continue to shape my life decades later. To be honest, I don't always trust myself. While my heart wants to make healthy choices, my flesh doesn't always want to do what is right or good.

Leaders are only as strong as the people who surround them. If we are to lead effectively and authentically, then we need healthy relationships that meet our personal and emotional needs. We also need one or two individuals who are willing to celebrate our accomplishments and successes without feeling inferior or resentful. It's natural for us to want to surround ourselves with people who think we're great, but not everyone in our inner circle needs to believe us invincible. We must round out our circle with those who are willing to brave the fire and call us out when we mess up.

We discussed Moses' leadership earlier in this book, and we know that he is the famed leader who guided millions of people through tumultuous seasons. And while it seemed as if Moses' leadership was thriving, his father-in-law, Jethro, discerned the toll of the emotional and mental stress placed on Moses. In a move of compassion, Jethro stepped in and explained to Moses that if he was going to continue leading successfully, then he would have to delegate the bulk of his responsibilities. Jethro wisely advised him to set in place seventy judges who would free up Moses' schedule by managing jurisdictional disagreements (Exodus 18).

As Jethro did for Moses, those who know us best will wave the warning flag to keep us from crumbling beneath the weight of external pressures. If you have someone who is willing to wade in and watch out for you and your well-being, embrace that person and count yourself among the blessed.

If you are a football fan, then you know that the guard position is made up of players who protect the offensive line. An effective guard doesn't mind stepping in harm's way to shield his teammates. As leaders, we need that kind of protection; we need colleagues who will run interference for us while we try to pick up yards and move in the right direction. We also need gatekeepers who keep critics at bay and guard our influence.

Leading is challenging enough without the voices of those who claim to be on our team but covertly work against us. The last thing we need is to be emotionally ambushed by those within our tribe. One example of this is Phil, a contractor and multi-millionaire. On the surface, his life seemed perfect. But during a private conversation with me, he shared some of his more difficult times. He said, "At my lowest point, I would visit an elderly woman who was like a mother to me. When I was frustrated over a business deal that had gone wrong or needed to talk through a personal matter, I would have coffee with her at her home. Even though she did not understand the intricate details of how my business operated, she listened closely and gave me space to express my feelings. Although she never offered any advice, I left her presence feeling like I could move mountains." We all need a safe place to sit and spill out our feelings.

We need more than just the soft-spoken person to speak into our lives. Sometimes we need people to redirect our sights off ourselves. It's all too easy to get caught up on our achievements, titles, and good remarks, but we must guard our hearts and take a hard look at the areas that still need work. It's not comfortable for someone to bust open our ego. It took me longer to listen to my critics than my cheerleaders.

Do you have someone in your life who sends warning shots when your behavior threatens to ruin your character? Do you feel secure enough to let someone step in and speak words that feel more sharp than smooth? As I think about the rewards that come with having a humble heart, I am reminded of the words Paul wrote from prison: "Don't be selfish; don't try to impress others. Be humble, thinking of others as better than yourselves" (Philippians 2:3 NLT).

Every leader needs a faithful coworker who will stand shoulder to shoulder when things start to fall apart. The apostle Paul found this depth of friendship in Silas, who shared in his suffering for the cause of Christ. Just hours after being thrown into prison for preaching the gospel, Paul and Silas linked arms and led their own private worship service. I don't know about you, but if I found myself incarcerated, I don't think singing would be among the things I'd do to pass the time. Finding strength in each other's plight, Paul and Silas lifted their voices, and their hymns stirred the hearts of other prisoners who listened in the dark. I pray that God will send you Silas-quality relationships and friends who stick by you through tough times, refusing to cast shade on your celebrations.

Truett Cathy, the founder of Chick-fil-A, once told an audience, "You know how you can tell if somebody needs encouragement?" He continued, "If they are breathing."[23] Whether you lead a group of toddlers or corporate executives, the weight of pointing others in the right direction can be a heavy assignment. Most leaders long for covenant friends who come alongside them without criticism or competition.

It's not often that you can find strong-willed men who are willing to fight through life together. In fact, it is usually the brave and confident ones who end up as foes rather than friends. But on a rare occasion, the pages of history let us glimpse into the lives of men who lived like brothers. On a worn piece of parchment written around 630 BCE is the story of two men who were willing to give up their lives for each other. Jonathan, the son of a king, and David, the son of a shepherd, were thrown together in a script that only heaven could construct. Even though David became Jonathan's brother-in-law, it wasn't their family ties that forced them together but rather their commitment to watch over each other. I encourage you to flip to their story in the book of 1 Samuel. It is a moving saga of shared solidarity that I want to highlight.

In the middle of the book of Samuel, we find David running away from Jonathan's father, King Saul. David wasn't running because he had done anything wrong but because the king was having a mental meltdown. By the time we reach this passage, bouts of paranoia and days of depression had pushed Saul to his emotional tipping point. His manic behavior had him tossing spears at David and anyone who tried to defend him. Few of us know the anguish of having our father plan to assassinate our friends.

Fearing for David's life, Jonathan crept away from the castle long enough to meet with his friend. When he found David, this is what happened: "Jonathan made a solemn pact with David, because he loved him as he loved himself. Jonathan sealed the pact by taking off his robe and giving it to David, together with his tunic, sword, bow, and belt" (1 Samuel 18:3–4 NLT).

In the modern world, what Jonathan did may seem strange if not insignificant. But in their time and culture, Jonathan's act of giving David his clothes and weapons was a symbolic act of brotherhood. It meant Jonathan released his right to become king and transferred it to David. I imagine it must have been a bittersweet moment for these brothers to know that this one act of love would change history. Jonathan was humble enough to honor his friend above himself. It wasn't a small gesture that David soon forgot. No, to a man like David, it became a memory that would carve out their destinies, and the results of their covenant lasted long after they passed away.

Trustworthiness is not a trait that you gain overnight, and I admit that I don't know many men who love each other enough to hand over their businesses or kingdoms. Many years ago, a friend gave me some advice that I still rely on today. She said, "Share information that you don't mind someone repeating and see if it gets back to you. Over time, you learn who you can trust." After a few bad experiences, I learned to stop sharing information with people who failed this truth test. I know that may sound harsh or judgmental, but even Jesus metaphorically warned his disciples about throwing pearls of truth before pigs (Matthew 7:6).

Not everyone can be trusted with valuable information. In fact, Jesus divided his followers into groups according to how much he trusted them. When speaking to the masses, he used generic illustrations. With his followers, he hid truths within parables, and when alone with his disciples, he shared kingdom principles. Within his inner circle of three—Peter, James, and John—he spoke of mysteries. And with John, the disciple whom he loved, he confided the truths that we read in Revelation. Like all influential leaders, Jesus reserved the highest level of truth for those he trusted most.

During a church service, a pastor who shall remain nameless challenged those attending to take their wallet and hand it to the person behind them. The request triggered laughter, but not a single wallet passed between hands. A simple request highlighted the fact that most people are unwilling to trust others with their money. After all the financial scandals that have surfaced over the last few decades, I'm leery of handing off my wallet too.

Some years ago, a news anchor did a piece on Bernard Madoff, who died in prison while serving out a 150-year sentence. The Bernard L. Madoff Investment Securities, LLC, scandal remains one of America's greatest financial crises. Bernie Madoff was an innovator in electronic trading and a former chairman of the Nasdaq. A legend in finance, Madoff was a trusted economic strategist and profitable investor. It would take nearly seventeen years before the world would discover that Madoff was the mastermind behind a global Ponzi scheme that defrauded billions of dollars from thousands of investors.

How did Madoff's company end up in financial ruin? Over the years Madoff claimed that investors could generate large and sustained returns on securities investments. Instead of following public trading guidelines and investing money in secure accounts, Madoff placed his clients' funds in one large account. He would take money invested by new clients and use it to pay existing clients large dividends on their returns. This cycle of funneling investments worked until the financial markets took a downward turn in 2008. Then, Madoff's clients requested $7 billion in payout withdrawals. This amount far exceeded the $200–300 million in the company's reserves.

Discovery of his crimes came to light when he confessed the truth to his sons, and they turned him in to local authorities. During an interview, he admitted he did not know why he committed the crime. Lack of character cost him more than a prison sentence. The guilt of stealing thousands of people's financial security was only the tip of the iceberg. Those nearest to him, especially his family, were also affected. Ruth Madoff, his wife and childhood sweetheart, said, "It was something that not in a million years I would have expected." Mark Madoff, his eldest son, hanged himself two years to the day after his father's confession. His younger son, Andy, died at the age of forty-eight from cancer. [24]

Trust was something Bernie Madoff used to build a multi-billion-dollar business, yet he lost it all. I imagine that if he had surrounded himself with people who would have held him accountable for his actions, that business would have proceeded with honesty and integrity. If Madoff was intelligent enough to build an illegal business, then surely he was brilliant enough to run a legitimate one. I challenge all leaders to monitor and assess our trustworthiness and the trustworthiness of those around us.

A famous quote says, "Show me your friends, and I will show you your future." Whether you realize it or not, your friends are a declaration of who you are and who you are becoming. Winners hang out with achievers. Dreamers spend time with creative thinkers. Critics sit around and gossip with cynics. You get the idea. Those closest to you are those who influence you the most. Today, take some time and make sure your relationships are a good match for your goals.

Trust me, we can't always discern the motives of those around us. Sometimes wolves disguised in sheep's clothing slip through the cracks. When they do, our first responsibility is to fight forward and find a way to forgive. I know it is not always easy to mend broken trust, and the truth is, some relationships will never fully recover. Just because someone apologizes for his or her actions doesn't mean that trust is automatically reinstated. It takes time and commitment for trust to be gained once it has been lost. I learned it is far easier to never let my trust be broken.

As I type the word *trust*, I cannot help but think of the word *betrayal,* its antonym. So often, a simple act of betrayal has turned *good people* into *bitter people.* Every leader has experienced the harsh truth that there are those within their camp who have acted graciously but are inwardly godless. Just this last month I talked with a leader who found out a man in his inner circle had tried to undermine his authority in order to take over his position. This wasn't the first time a corporate climber had tried to use his influence as a stepladder. I wish he were the only leader I've heard complain about disloyalty. Even those names we would list as part of our trusted inner circle can slip through the loop of loyalty and end up in the bucket of betrayers. Consider that Judas betrayed Jesus for a few coins and some clout within the religious circles.

One of my favorite quotes on leadership is by Sam Chand who said, "Loyalty earned is a beautiful thing, but loyalty demanded is toxic."[25] I agree that loyalty is not gained quickly but is earned over time. A quick way to test the loyalty of those in your camp is to watch how they respond to the failure, setbacks, mistakes, and harsh words of others. Someone once said, "Blood makes you related; loyalty makes you family." Loyalty is the litmus test of trust.

From one leader to another, I caution you to safeguard the trust of those who are dependable and dedicated. My friend, Samantha, recently shared that one of her closest confidants, Abby, had begun acting rather standoffish at the office. After spending a few days trying to figure out what was going on, Samantha asked Abby out for coffee.

Once they were settled, Samantha gathered the strength to ask what was wrong. In a cautious but honest way, Abby reminded Samantha of how Samantha had carelessly spoken about her in a recent board meeting. As the conversation proceeded, Abby's anger increased. Clenching her jaw, she leaned forward and said, "When are you going to get it? When are you going to learn we want to please you? We are not the enemy. We are not against you because we have a difference of opinion."

Samantha bit her lip when the words she had used in the board meeting were repeated back to her. It was a horrible mistake. She apologized for her demoralizing words and expressed deep regret. She went on to explain that she had been raised to believe that if someone publicly disagrees with you, then they are considered disloyal. After an hour of conversation, they were able to push through the issues and reconcile. Samantha learned how to embrace a difference of opinion without tying it to loyalty and found that successful leadership gives others the ability to air differences without feeling embattled.

Honor is not a topic that will head up most leadership teachings. In fact, it is one of the most overlooked subjects of modern society. When I mention honor, I'm not referring to the shallow platitudes of social climbers but rather the heartfelt actions of those who want to demonstrate gratitude. Not long ago my thoughts drifted to the story of King David's men who set out to honor him in a significant way. If you remember the tale in 2 Samuel 23:13–17, then you know it reads like a modern war movie. The Scripture passage reveals that when David expressed his desire for a drink of water, three of his best soldiers went behind enemy lines to retrieve water from a well that was twelve miles away. It doesn't sound like the kind of thing that would necessarily garner a medal of honor unless we understand the kind of danger that they subjected themselves to in order to make it happen. David would never have made this kind of request; he would have put a stop to the mission the second he heard about it.

Now imagine David's face when his soldiers presented him with the canteen of water. I'm sure the blood must have drained from his face when he realized they had risked their lives to grant his simple wish. David, overwhelmed with gratitude, turned the container upside down and let the liquid run out and pool on the ground as an offering to the Lord. The mutual respect that David shared with his soldiers is the kind of unity that made them invincible in battle and undivided in loyalty.

8

Practice Distance

The year 2020 will be remembered for the ominous changes _Threatening_ that COVID-19 forced upon our lives. The world was altered as we were forced into a "new normal." Never in modern human history had the world shut down without warning. Sports complexes, churches, schools, restaurants, and businesses were suddenly empty and large gatherings forbidden. An eerie feeling swept across the globe as movement in major cities came to a crawl. The world scrambled for answers, and many experts believed the best method of preventing the virus was to impose the practice of social distancing. Those who were exposed to the virus were encouraged to quarantine for fourteen days.

In a similar way, toxic relationships sometimes require us to "socially distance" or pull away from unhealthy individuals or environments. That doesn't necessarily mean we must permanently sever all ties with a person, but sometimes it's helpful to gradually distance ourselves from unhealthy relationships, particularly those that prove detrimental to our future. It's a hard truth, but not everyone we love is destined to be part of our future.

Remaining in toxic relationships opens the door to needless pain. False guilt attempts to fool us into going against our gut and bypassing what we believe to be true about others. I cannot tell you the number of times that the word *if* has caused setbacks and heartaches: "*If* only I'd stayed in the relationship longer; *if* I made them happier; *if* I made more money." If we are not mindful of the *if* factor, it will imprison our minds long past the time when we should have begun moving forward.

The greatest relationships on the earth should flow from the heart of family, and yet it's often the family unit that's most fragmented. Family members who work together face even greater challenges, as far too often, they are the first to acknowledge each other's failures and the last to celebrate each other's successes. The Gospel of Mark exemplifies just how difficult it is to win over the hearts of family members—even if you are as perfect as Jesus. Mark wrote that Jesus' brothers scoffed at Jesus while the rest of the world celebrated him. Even his sisters resented him and refused to believe in him, offended by his teachings. Feeling the criticism, Jesus wisely said, "A prophet is honored everywhere except in his hometown and among his relatives and his own family" (Mark 6:3–4 NLT).

Jesus' contemporaries knew about the events surrounding his birth, but they did not understand his supernatural origin.

They knew he was raised in the rural town of Nazareth, but that region was looked down upon as inferior. When Jesus began teaching publicly, theologians questioned the source of his wisdom and knowledge because he had not attended rabbinical schools. And Jesus almost knocked the world off its axis by proclaiming he was the Son of God. In fact, when Jesus brought his disciples to Nazareth, his family was less than welcoming: "The crowd gathered again, so that they could not even eat. And when his family heard it, they went out to seize him, for they were saying, 'He is out of his mind'" (Mark 3:20–21 ESV). Those who imagined they knew Jesus best described him as mentally unstable. If you have relatives who have undermined your worth, then you probably understand the scenario Jesus found himself in.

Jesus' family didn't take note of his fame until word spread of his good works. In an effort to push through the throng, they sent word to Jesus that they were among the crowd. Although the Bible doesn't record his physical reaction, I imagine Jesus took a few deep breaths before asking his disciples, "'Who is my mother? Who are my brothers?' Then he pointed to his disciples and said, 'Look, these are my mother and brothers. Anyone who does the will of my Father in heaven is my brother and sister and mother!'" (Matthew 12:47–50 NLT). Jesus made it clear that family is often the first to jump in line at even the slightest hint of fame. They'll request a private audience, hint at a handout, and fight for favor.

In dealing with corporations and churches, I have found that bowing to egotistical expectations breeds a culture of low morale. Privilege and promotion are rewards to be earned, not things to which we're entitled. If we revisit Jesus' answer to "Who is my family?," his response was crystal clear: "Anyone who does the will of my Father." Jesus set a relationship boundary based on brotherhood, not blood. Outsiders became insiders.

Not to belabor Bible stories in this chapter, but I feel that we cannot move forward without considering the family dynamics of Moses. In the book of Numbers, we find a passage that purposefully highlights family dysfunction:

> Miriam and Aaron spoke against Moses because of the Cushite woman whom he had married, for he had married a Cushite woman. And they said, "Has the LORD indeed spoken only through Moses? Has he not spoken through us also?" And the LORD heard it. Now the man Moses was very meek, more than all people who were on the face of the earth. And suddenly, the LORD said to Moses and to Aaron and Miriam, "Come out, you three, to the tent of meeting." And the three of them came out. And the LORD came down in a pillar of cloud and stood at the entrance of the tent and called Aaron and Miriam, and they both came forward. And he said, "Hear my words: If there is a prophet among you, I the LORD make myself known to him in a vision; I speak with him in a dream. Not so with my servant Moses. He is faithful in all my house. With him

I speak mouth to mouth, clearly, and not in riddles, and he beholds the form of the LORD. Why then were you not afraid to speak against my servant Moses?" And the anger of the LORD was kindled against them, and he departed.

When the cloud removed from over the tent, behold, Miriam was leprous, like snow. And Aaron turned toward Miriam, and behold, she was leprous. And Aaron said to Moses, "Oh, my lord, do not punish us because we have done foolishly and have sinned. Let her not be as one dead, whose flesh is half eaten away when he comes out of his mother's womb." And Moses cried to the LORD, "O God, please heal her— please." But the LORD said to Moses, "If her father had but spit in her face, should she not be shamed seven days? Let her be shut outside the camp seven days, and after that she may be brought in again." (Numbers 12:1–14 ESV)

The line about her father spitting in her face clearly spells out the direction this story is heading. As we tumble through this tale, remember that Moses was God's chosen leader, Aaron was Moses' brother, and Miriam his sister. Also keep in mind that they were appointed to facilitate Moses' leadership, not criticize it. In a way that was totally disrespectful, they called Moses' character on the mat in front of the very people who revered him. And if we study their family dynamics, it is easy to see that Aaron didn't support Moses' decision, and Miriam likely felt threatened by Moses' wife. After all, Miriam had been a prominent female figure in Israel's history, and making room for other leaders is not something leaders typically do naturally.

Before we push forward, let's read the text once more to identify key phrases that allude to fractures within the family. In one question, Moses' siblings reveal the nature of their spiritual condition: "Has God spoken only through you?" I can assure you that those words were not spoken softly. They probably roared like the sound of a jet engine, and their accusations revealed the depth of their jealousy. Although the passage doesn't explain the root of their jealousy, we can speculate. Perhaps some of it was because Moses was the youngest sibling, or the fact that Moses was married, while Miriam was not. Whatever the reason behind their bitterness, one thing is for sure: Their accomplishments were small compared to the accomplishments of Moses. Moses was a CEO, a general, a judge, and a visionary. Aaron was his elder, but he echoed whatever Moses said. One brother carved out the Ten Commandments, and the other carved out a calf to worship (Exodus 32).

It is always dangerous to go against that which God endorses. When God heard murmurings against Moses, he responded resolutely. In a voice that shook the earth, God asked, "Why were you not afraid to speak against my servant?" That sentence should make us second-guess insubordination. God did more than question their actions; he leveled the dishonorable with leprosy. In a scene from a horror movie, Miriam's skin turns white, and her flesh recedes. Driven to the outskirts of town, her sin separated her from society. Forced social distancing gave her time to reflect on her actions and repent her disrespect.

Sometimes we need social separation not because of criticism but because individuals may overstep or waste our time. During an interview Dan Rather conducted with Vince Gill, a Country Music Hall of Fame inductee, Rather asked Gill about his anger issues. Owning up to his actions, Gill shared that his bouts with his temper showed up on the golf course more than anywhere else. Gill further explained that his counselor explained to him why the golf course was such a trigger for his anger: "Vince, you have surrounded yourself with *yes* people. You constantly hear comments like, 'That was perfect! You're the best. You did a great job. It can't be done better than that.'" Whenever he hit a bad shot, Gill lost his cool. He realized that the yes people he had surrounded himself with were wasting his time. He also came to understand that sometimes his shot wasn't the best, and like everyone else, they occasionally fell far from the green.[26] We limit our growth when we surround ourselves with people who only tell us what we want to hear.

Another reason we may want to socially distance ourselves from others is if our core values do not align. Numerous blog sites and countless statistics consider this lack of shared values as a predictive trait of a failed relationship. Resentment and friction tend to form when friendships or business associates have opposing ethics. Another common trait among fractured friendships is a one-sided relationship in which one person puts in the majority of effort. I am sure you could make a list of individuals who suck the life right out of the room or drain you of your energy.

For years I had a friend who was only content when everyone else was miserable. When a project was proposed at work, her critical comments destroyed any hope of creativity flourishing. Although she was brilliant, her cynicism and superiority complex left colleagues begging to join other teams. She brought the dark cloud she lived underneath into every room she entered yet had no idea why people pulled away from her.

Over the years, I have learned that time is one of my greatest commodities. It ranks high on my list of things that I diligently guard. I encourage you to evaluate how others engage with and affect you when you spend your time with them. Are they mentally present during your conversations? Are they disrespectful, self-absorbed, multi-tasking, or emotionally disconnected when they ask for a slice of your time? Are you respectful of other people's time? Taking note of these small nuances in yourself and in others will help you identify hidden, subtle traits that could prove disastrous down the road.

Stealthy people know how to conceal their more unsavory traits and tend not to show their malicious sides until it is too late to recover from the damages. If you have watched the movie *The Lion King*, then you know how crafty disloyal people can behave. It took fatalities for Simba to recognize that his uncle, Scar, was maniacal and manipulative. How many times do we write off the schemes of others as unintentional coincidences? One of the most dangerous relationships we can experience is one with someone who applauds us publicly but undermines us privately. Some colleagues are notorious for affirming ideas in the boardroom only to systematically dismantle them behind closed doors. They scavenge for negatives in a world full of positives. It is time that, like Simba, we recognize our own strength and remove power and authority from those who would impede our progress or discourage our potential. Not only is it a wise decision, but it's also a biblical one. Paul's letter to Titus cautions, "As for a person who stirs up division, after warning him once and then twice, have nothing more to do with him" (Titus 3:10 ESV).

When we tolerate bad behavior, we encourage it. Rarely will it change or improve with time. Like drinking water from poisoned wells, those who consume contamination eventually become sick themselves. In short, toxic personalities negatively affect team morale. To return to the story of Moses, Aaron and Miriam tried to veil their criticism as if they were being open and honest, when in reality it was a setup to air their grievances and insecurities.

Smart leaders are quick to spot the difference between team members who want to share ideas and those who want to shake down those in charge. An open environment in the workplace creates freedom to safely talk about issues without throwing others under the bus. Just because someone couches their criticism with the word *transparency* does not transform their hurtful comments into helpful ones. Pay attention to the delivery of colleagues' comments, not just the words they weave together. If a person consistently fuses his or her words in a way that leaves others feeling more controlled than empowered, or more discouraged than encouraged, then they may be masquerading their manipulation as openness.

Leaders struggle to sever ties with unhealthy people. That's why there are so many upper-level business courses designed to train executives on how to terminate subordinates with minimal corporate trauma. CEOs know from experience that risk is involved in terminating an employee as well as bringing one on board.

A teacher named Kimberly called a meeting with Grayson, the school superintendent, to complain about repeated incidents with Tom, a popular teacher. She cited that Tom had made several sexual advances toward her. When Grayson confronted Tom about the accusations, Tom firmly denied them. Knowing the seriousness of the allegations against Tom, Kimberly set up a second meeting with Grayson and brought the principal along as a witness. The interaction during the meeting was carefully documented, and Kimberly provided a verbal testimony. During this second confrontation, Tom sheepishly admitted he was guilty. Grayson assured Tom that the reason for his dismissal would not be made public under the condition that Tom did not fabricate reasons for his termination.

Instead of keeping his word, Tom told his wife that he had been fired because another teacher had falsely accused him. In an outburst of anger, his wife went to Grayson about her husband's termination. Because Tom broke his promise, Grayson and the principal read to her the account of the meeting that took place with Tom. Tom's wife's face went pale, and her demeanor changed. She apologized for her actions and left in tears. At the next school board meeting, the transcript of Tom's verbal confession was read aloud as well as the recorded conversation of Tom's agreement to the terms for dismissal. Like many leaders throughout the ages, Tom tried to conceal his actions in order to get his way. He longed for his transgressions to be swept under the rug.

Whenever difficult conversations must take place, whether it's terminating an employee, providing constructive feedback, or distancing from an unhealthy relationship or environment, I have learned to minimize the risks by constructing safe spaces in which to hold these difficult conversations. In my company, for example, one of our policies is to make sure that terminations are conducted in person, at least three individuals are present as witnesses, and the proceedings are documented and recorded. This provides a safety net for situations that might prove volatile or combative. It's a difficult process, but it doesn't have to be conducted in a detrimental way. Set the tone for how you want the scene to unfold. Be wise, exercise caution, remain focused, and stick to the issue at hand.

9

Guard Your Wellness

When I heard the horrible news about Amelia, my heart sank into my shoes. The news of her suicide made headlines, and everyone struggled to see the heartache they had all missed. For years she had served as the CEO of a major corporation. As a leader, she was driven, highly motivated, and successful. Everything in her life appeared to be moving in the right direction, but the hidden truth was that Amelia waged a silent war with ongoing bouts of mental illness. Fearing to let her colleagues and friends know about her condition, she pushed anxiety to the side and fought to normalize her emotions. No one knew of her private struggle because she didn't let anyone get close enough to peer behind the veil of fear. For weeks everyone asked the obvious: *How could something like this happen to a woman everyone felt they knew so well?*

Amelia carried secrets. As a child, she suffered sexual abuse that left her infertile. In addition to her private pain was her recent discovery of her husband's affair. It wasn't a secret romance that could be pushed to the side; the affair made office headlines. She heard her name whispered among the gossip, and the room hushed whenever she walked in. When it came out that her husband was cheating with one of her close friends, Amelia's personality began to change. She lost energy and enthusiasm. Work that she had always turned in on time was now late, and she offered no explanation or excuse. Some days she ate continually, and other days she skipped meals altogether. The signs were subtle but present nonetheless. I often wonder if life would have turned out differently if someone had taken the time to check in with her as a person, not just a professional.

We are blind to the private battles of those who lead the way. My heart grows heavy when I think about men and women who have mentally or emotionally crumbled because they could not reach out for counseling or therapy. Instead, they determined to deal with the pressure alone and tried to press forward. Society has attempted to convince us that executives should be the ones guiding, not grieving. Even the words *leader* and *mental illness* do not seem to go together. Too often, leaders are emotionally crippled by the time people start to care. I've lost track of the number of opportunities I've missed to help someone out of a dark situation. It wasn't that I didn't see red flags or didn't want to help. The hard part was knowing how to initiate steps to bring about deliverance without pushing the person into even deeper darkness.

After watching some highly driven leaders nosedive into depression, I finally found ways to bring about help without creating more hurt. Maybe you know someone who needs help finding his or her way out of a dangerous place. If so, I encourage you to make a list of your concerns. Write down and date any actions or responses that may seem out of character for this individual. If you need to address some concerns, rehearse what you will say and how you will say it before approaching them. Nothing is worse than letting the wrong words slip out when your heart is in the right place. I've learned to bring to the table only what is honest and accurate. Then present the facts in a way that comes across as noncombative or critical.

As a leader, how you deal with problems speaks volumes about your character and ability to resolve ongoing issues. I once employed a man who was chronically late to meetings and neglected to turn his projects in on time. While it's not in the same vein as mental illness, it was a personal issue that needed to be addressed. One day over lunch, I explained that his lack of discipline not only affected his work but also those who worked on his team. It took a while, but I was finally able to get him to see how his apathetic attitude was creating a roadblock for the entire staff. I realize not all problems can be solved over a sandwich. Sometimes serious infractions require the involvement of professional help. Some situations may require a mental health expert to address the issue. I know of more than one CEO who benefited from taking a leave of absence to gain a fresh outlook.

Reed Hastings, CEO of Netflix, takes six weeks of vacation a year. He says, "You often do your best thinking when you're off hiking in some mountain…and you get a different perspective on something."[27] Richard Branson, founder of the Virgin Group, said:

> Maintaining focus on having fun isn't just about rest and recuperation: When you go on vacation, your routine is interrupted; the places you go and the new people you meet can inspire you in unexpected ways. As an entrepreneur or business leader, if you didn't come back from your vacation with some ideas about how to shake things up, it's time to consider making some changes. I make sure that I disconnect by leaving my smartphone at home or in the hotel room for as long as possible—days, if I can—and bringing a notepad and pen with me instead. Freed from the daily stresses of my working life, I find that I am more likely to have new insights into old problems and other flashes of inspiration.[28]

Marissa Mayer, CEO of Yahoo!, takes a week's vacation every four months.[29] Megachurch pastor Robert Morris takes a three-month sabbatical each year. He teaches that creativity and freshness come more during the times he is not focused on producing.

In the past, extended vacations or sabbaticals were uncommon. When leaders cannot get rested and relaxed, stress and tension can push them to a breaking point. I know of a pastor who retired after thirty years of ministry only to have a nervous breakdown at the age of seventy-seven. That man was my father. Publicly he was strong, funny, and possessed a natural quick wit. But the emotional pain he had shoved deep inside came to the surface later in life. I remember the stress being so intense that his body broke out in hives. On multiple occasions, his lips, face, and feet would swell to twice their normal size. He spontaneously broke into tears and suffered recurring nightmares that robbed him of restful sleep.

After we took him to a trusted psychiatrist, they informed us that he struggled with latent childhood abuse. As a young boy, he couldn't focus in class because of the physical and verbal abuse he suffered from his alcoholic father. The ongoing trauma of watching his father abuse his mother shut down parts of him that would never live again. And to complicate an already burdensome home life, he was the second oldest of nine children and forced to work on the farm while his younger siblings attended school. Academically he never advanced beyond fifth grade. Lacking a sufficient education proved problematic for him as a leader. Years of feeling inferior eroded his self-confidence, and insecurity became an internal source of torment.

After long counseling sessions, the medical team prescribed medication to help my father live out the remainder of his days with some modicum of peace. I regret not being able to get my dad to a doctor before his breakdown. The thing is that despite all of his inward issues, he was a successful leader and pastor. After almost five decades of observing and assisting leaders, I have discovered that the number of clergy members who struggle with mental health issues is staggeringly high. It is disproportionately higher than other professions. A recent study conducted by Lifeway Research revealed that 23 percent of pastors admitted they had battled a mental illness,[30] and yet the church seems to have fallen silent on the issue. If we are to win the war against mental illness, we must trace back the causes of psychiatric problems and bring reliable solutions to the table.

Just like any other organ within the body, the mind can develop serious illnesses or diseases. Maybe you or someone you know is like my dad, who shoves away issues instead of dealing with them on the surface. The first step to overcoming trauma is admitting that you are struggling. Trust me when I say that denial does not change or dissolve our experiences; it drags them into our future. Like a heavy anchor, denial lets us trudge forward. It weighs us down in ways we cannot see, forbidding us from flying freely into the next season of our lives.

If you or someone you know is walking through a difficult season, reach out for help. Psychiatric help, medication, therapy, and spiritual counseling can help us settle issues that leave us feeling isolated and alone. One of my favorite quotes is from Glenn Close, who said, "What mental health needs are more sunlight, more candor, and more unashamed conversation."[31] I have found that conversation brings understanding to the table of healing. On the other hand, secrecy is often the silent trigger that fires off rounds of gossip, speculation, and misinformation. By being open and transparent about your needs, you allow others to take part in your healing journey. Fred Rogers, who was known for his ability to gently tap into the human soul, once said, "When we can talk about our feelings, they become less overwhelming, less upsetting, and less scary. The people we trust with that important talk can help us know that we're not alone."[32]

A professor at the University of California San Francisco (UCSF) surveyed 242 entrepreneurs regarding their mental health. Of those surveyed, a whopping 49 percent recorded having a mental health issue they dealt with daily. The illness that ranked highest among these business leaders was depression, followed closely by attention-deficit/hyperactivity disorder (ADHD) and anxiety.[33] The dictionary defines *depression* as "a mental condition characterized by feelings of severe despondency and dejection."[34] It is not uncommon for feelings of inadequacy and guilt to accompany a lack of energy, loss of appetite, or sleep disruption. Depression may be associated with bipolar disorder, mania, and extreme mood swings and has been known to affect many postpartum mothers.

As I think back over my conversations with strong leaders, I realize how many of them were willing to table their feelings to appease others. But if frustration and anger are not released in a healthy, productive way, those emotions turn inward and attack our physical and psychological health. It is a well-documented fact that many mental health experts link depression to high anxiety and anger levels. Although today's culture has gained a better understanding of how unresolved emotions create negative thought processes, many high-profile leaders still struggle to find healthy ways to process their complex emotions.

It is essential to understand how to release emotions that may otherwise compromise or damage our mental health. I recently used an ordinary object to illustrate this point. I invited the man I was counseling to look at a deflated balloon. As he stared in silence, I explained that our emotional chambers should mirror the balloon in many ways. I asked him, "What would happen if I were to take the balloon and stretch it or stomp on it?"

After thinking through the idea, the man said, "I suppose nothing would happen."

I agreed. "It would not lose its shape but would return to being relaxed and flexible," I explained. "What do you think would happen if I were to force too much air into the balloon?"

"Eventually, it would explode," he answered.

I smiled and nodded. My point was to draw attention to the fact that any time we push our emotional chambers beyond their capacities, they eventually burst. The only kind of person who cannot feel their emotions is a dead one. We feel the full impact of our emotions whether we consciously recognize it or not. If we are to live out our days healthy and productively, we must embrace, acknowledge, and process emotions before they violently erupt. The key to releasing anger or anxiety without creating harm is slowly letting the pain loose and not letting it accumulate excessive pressure. In a similar way to releasing a cork from a bottle, emotions are to be released slowly over time.

Last week I thought of a young lady who grew up suffering verbal abuse from her father. From childhood well into adult life, she was labeled, belittled, and given no affection. During an intense counseling session, she agreed to forgive her father. After she verbally released him, I asked her to take an object and destroy it as a method of releasing her suppressed anger. I asked her while walking through this exercise to speak words to her father that she had been unable to articulate before that moment. At first, she expressed her words in a soft voice, and then with each passing sentence, her voice rose until she was screaming out her words. When she completed the exercise, she was exhausted but also at peace.

One of the most comforting words spoken is the word *peace*. God's plan for your life is that you live in peace. Depression wants us to believe that God is not for us, that he's disconnected from our feelings or absent from the tragedies in our lives. The opposite is true, although it's possible that we shut God out of the hidden places within our hearts. One of my favorite verses on peace is in the book of Isaiah: "You will keep in perfect peace all who trust in you, all whose thoughts are fixed on you!" (Isaiah 26:3 NLT). In dark seasons, we spend our energy looking for a way out rather than seeking the one who can turn on the light. Another passage expresses the idea of looking to our Creator for help this way: "Because of the multitude of oppressions people cry out; they call for help because of the arm of the mighty. But none says, 'Where is God my Maker, who gives songs in the night'" (Job 35:9–10 ESV).

One of the most remarkable soothing techniques for anxiety is listening to music. According to a study by Finnish researchers published in the British Journal of Psychiatrists, "Music therapy plus standard care shows a steady improvement in depressive symptoms among the depressed than those just receiving standard care. It helps improve the general wellbeing of individuals, as well."[35] The book of 1 Samuel tells how King Saul calmed his restless heart during a time in which an oppressive spirit troubled him by sending for a psalmist to play music throughout the palace. History revealed that as David's music filled the chambers, the dark spirits departed from Saul. I believe this is an accurate account, as I, too, have watched music soothe troubled souls and bring hope to the hurting. Music is a mysterious but powerful link that connects our hearts to our Creator. Music therapy is commonly listed among healing techniques for victims of trauma.

Positive meditation is another technique that can prove effective in calming our thoughts and emotions. Any time we focus our thoughts on God's Word, we bring order to our feelings, strengthen our faith, and discover hope. If you are not already reading and meditating on Scripture, I encourage you to carve out and reserve at least twenty minutes each day to direct your thoughts. Giving direction to our thoughts is not always easy to accomplish. Maybe that is why I am in awe of the apostle Paul, who from a darkened prison cell found the strength to write these words: "Whatever is true, whatever is honorable, whatever is just, whatever is pure, whatever is lovely, whatever is commendable, if there is any excellence, if there is anything worthy of praise, think about these things...and the God of peace will be with you" (Philippians 4:8–9 ESV).

When leaders come to me for advice, I am quick to have them pinpoint their emotions. After coffee and casual conversation, I ask them to define how they feel using only one word. More than I like to admit, their answer is "exhaustion." When I think of leaders who were both effective and borderline exhausted, my mind drifts to the prophet Elijah. If you were to

Google Elijah's name or read the entry on Wikipedia, you would find information like: "Defended the worship of the Hebrew God over that of the Canaanite deity Baal. God also performed many miracles through Elijah, including resurrection (raising the dead), bringing fire down from the sky, and entering heaven alive 'by fire.'"[36] But if you continued to read, you would discover that threats from a power-hungry queen sent him running into the wilderness to hide (1 Kings 19).

In a way that is not uncommon for leaders to behave, Elijah goes from having a powerful run at things to feeling powerless. On more than one occasion, Elijah curls up in a cave, suffering from suicidal thoughts (see 1 Kings 19:4). If we were to trace the story back to what led him there, we would find that fatigue and frustration were contributing factors. I've learned that if we are to avoid the snare of depression, we have to pay attention to the warning signs flashing "Danger ahead!" It's time we stop and listen to what our bodies are trying to tell our minds.

In a blog that recently tumbled across my screen, I learned that psychiatric disorders rank high among our generation's most artistic and creative leaders. Mania, for instance, is associated with creativity. Depression is associated with enhanced realism.[37] The truth is that both mania and depression may increase an inner determination and strength. Some of the world's most productive leaders in history struggled with mental illness.

President Abraham Lincoln fought clinical depression for most of his life. The poetry he quoted most contained dark, suicidal themes, and he confided to his closest friends that it would be easier for him to die than to live. To his law partner in

Washington, he wrote: "I am now the most miserable man living. If what I feel were equally distributed to the whole human family, there would not be one cheerful face on the earth. Whether I shall ever be better I cannot tell; I awfully forebode I shall not. To remain as I am is impossible; I must die or be better, it appears to me."[38] Yet even with all the inner conflict, Lincoln pushed forward to accomplish a monumental act that would transform history. He turned from the question of *whether he could* live to *how he would* live. Choosing to focus on what he wanted to be known for became his motivation for living. The same strength he gathered to battle depression would work in his favor as he crafted speeches, led an army, fought against slavery, and united a nation.

Most people would be surprised to know that Dr. Martin Luther King Jr., leader of the civil rights movement in the 1950s and 60s, attempted suicide two times before age twelve. At age fifteen, he enrolled at Morehouse College in Atlanta. He was a brilliant man and a formidable leader as an adult, yet his closest friends were concerned about his mental health toward the end of his life. They strongly encouraged him to seek professional help. The following quote from him is part of the legacy he left to the depressed and oppressed, and it's likely that he spoke from his private pain: "If you can't fly, then run. If you can't run, then walk. If you can't walk, then crawl. But whatever you do, you have to keep moving forward."[39] Other world leaders who fought private internal battles include John F. Kennedy, Prime Minister Winston Churchill, Mahatma Gandhi, and Diana Princess of Wales.[40] More times than not great leaders have suffered in silence.

Despite what society tries to force us into believing, a quick online self-help course does not bring lasting healing. The reality is that internal healing will take time and concentrated effort. I like how Beau Taplin sheds light on the subject: "I cannot stand the words 'Get over it.' All of us are under such pressure to put our problems in the past tense. Slow down. Don't allow others to hurry your healing. It is a process, one that may take years, occasionally, even a lifetime—and that's OK."[41]

As I think back over the lives of great men and women, I have concluded that owning our brokenness is the first, brave, powerful step toward restoration. With God's help, we can find our way and become better, more refined versions of who we once were. I will close out my thoughts and this chapter with a quote by J. M. Storm: "She is a beautiful piece of broken pottery, put back together by her own hands. And a critical world judges her cracks while missing the beauty of how she made herself whole again."[42]

10

Stay the Path of Freedom

I remember where I was when I read a social media post that ousted a high-profile ministry leader for his illegal drug use. At first, I thought it was a horrible joke or a malicious rumor, but when his arrest splashed across the nightly news, the truth began to sink in. Understandably, his family, friends, and community members had a difficult time wrapping their minds around the fact that this man was guilty of illegal activity. The question that continued to haunt the people that knew him best was how a man of such great influence could be a drug addict. After all, he was a mentor, a minister, and a highly respected leader.

When the truth came tumbling out, his addiction was traced back to medications prescribed for an injury. What began as a treatment for back pain grew into a full-blown opioid addiction.

I wish his story were an isolated one, but it's not. According to a 2018 report by the American Psychiatric Association, 5 percent of the adult population have abused or been addicted to opioids or prescription painkillers.[43] Far too many leaders end up losing the battle with addiction because they minimize the effects of legalized pharmaceuticals. Opioid addiction is an invisible enemy that slowly imprisons innocent people.

Our culture tends to rely on stereotypes to capture what a person with an addictive personality looks like. We might think of addicts as traumatized people who can't hold a job, keep a home, and have needle marks in their arms. Not only is this inaccurate, but it's also counterproductive when identifying those who are battling secret addictions. Chances are that each of us knows an individual or individuals who wrestled with addiction but whose lives appeared perfectly intact. Many high-profile individuals are well off, highly educated, and successful in their professions yet fight demons of addiction. For a while, their addiction may seem to enhance their ability to function at a high level, making it even more difficult for that person to recognize their problem and seek professional help.

Audrey Gelman, founder and CEO of The Wing, a co-working space for women, recently celebrated three years of sobriety. Austin Geidt, a high-ranking executive for Uber's Advanced Technologies Group, nearly threw away her college career because of a drug addiction. Media mogul Oprah Winfrey, who is worth billions of dollars, admits she struggled with a crack cocaine addiction as a young adult. Larry Kudlow, who served as an economic advisor for several US presidential administrations, was addicted to drugs and alcohol during the time he worked on Wall Street. Steve Madden, a designer of luxury fashion styles, said he laundered money and committed fraud to support his addiction to alcohol and drugs. CEO and cofounder of nonprofit Everytable, Sam Polk, says his addictions to alcohol and drugs started in college.[44] Some of these names might have caught you by surprise if for no other reason than their success, which shielded the general public from their battles with addiction.

I could tell you story after story of self-assured, successful people whose addictions eroded their self-confidence. I could also explain how addiction alters relationships and modifies individuals' nature, traits, and temperament. I had a sweet lady confide to me that alcohol so changed her husband's personality that she no longer recognized the man who shared her bed. What struck me to the core was when her husband said, "I've lived in an altered state of mind for so long that I'm afraid that if I sober up, then I won't like myself or love my wife." The truth was that he had cheated on his wife, not with another woman but with whiskey. He was devastated to realize that he had grown more emotionally attached to the bottle than to his bride.

When I was young, my father passed me on the interstate and challenged me to show off the speed of my new car. Not thinking about my wife and baby, who were in the car, I dropped my foot onto the accelerator and pushed it to the floor. For three or four miles, my dad and I raced side by side. Young and self-willed, I refused to fall behind, even if it meant receiving a sizable ticket or (even worse) endangering the lives of the ones I love. After a while, my dad finally backed down, and we both reduced our speed. It wasn't until I parked the car that I discovered large bubbles on my two front tires. If those bubbles had burst while I was racing recklessly down the highway, it could have cost my family their lives.

In much the same way, leaders tend to accelerate and push faster than they should to reach or maintain success. Very few know how to slow down, pull back, and face challenges at a healthy pace. Instead, they push the limits by working double time, taking unnecessary risks, and forfeiting rest. As a result, pressure builds up, and they forget that a blowout is imminent. I've held many heart-wrenching conversations with men and women who chose drugs or alcohol as a pick-me-up to push them through the pressure. What starts as an occasional boost to help them feel better or obtain more energy escalates until they lose complete control. Over time, the casual user becomes addicted, and it takes years for them to regain their footing.

The most descriptive way to explain the cycle of addiction is to imagine living in hell without a back door. Addiction sneaks its way in, offering a tempting opportunity to escape reality, explore sin, or evade consequences. It cripples the mind of the user, replacing healthy thoughts with toxic ones. It wears on the body, soul, and spirit of an individual, as the path of addiction is filled with guilt, lies, shame, and self-hate. These emotions become life-threatening because they encourage the addict to remain living in secrecy and denial.

At the root of addiction is a lie that tries to sell the idea that a substance is a solution when nothing could be further from the truth. However, it's interesting to note that some studies show that those who struggle with addiction may have similar characteristics in common: impulsive actions, risk-taking behaviors, difficulty delaying gratification, self-esteem issues, tolerance for deviant behavior, relationship insecurity, and anxiety or depressive episodes.[45] I have never met an addict who wanted to be bound by addiction. I have met people with great potential who pushed their ambitions too far and found themselves controlled by pills, powders, pornography, sex, and scandal. A man known for his words of wisdom describes the effects of addiction this way:

> Who has anguish? Who has sorrow? Who
> is always fighting? Who is always complain-
> ing? Who has unnecessary bruises? Who has
> bloodshot eyes? It is the one who spends long
> hours in the taverns, trying out new drinks.
> Don't gaze at the wine, seeing how red it is,
> how it sparkles in the cup, how smoothly it
> goes down. For in the end it bites like a poi-
> sonous snake; it stings like a viper. You will see
> hallucinations, and you will say crazy things.
> (Proverbs 23:29–33 NLT)

Pornography is exceptionally enticing. As access to pornography has increased, the stigma toward it has seemingly decreased. It's more accepted today than in previous decades—even among those who ascribe to religious beliefs. According to a *Christianity Today* survey, 40 percent of evangelical protestant leaders in the United States struggle with pornography.[46] Production of porn is designed to gain, keep, and alter the emotional and sensory parts of the mind. It is webbed together in a way that pulls the viewer into a fantasy world that is hard to escape. Journalist Julie Bindel described in a scathing article for *The Spectator* magazine how the industry has become mainstream, and she puts that greed into perspective: "Annual revenue from the global porn industry has been estimated at up to $90 billion...Hollywood makes about $10 billion a year."[47]

Those who have consumed large quantities of pornography often have trouble resisting inappropriate, tormented thoughts long after they escape their addiction. I know plenty of men and women who became addicts after just one click to a pornographic website. It took long, painful journeys for many of them to renew their minds and regain their purity. Countless other people have yet to pry themselves away from the trap that ensnared them. I'll share examples of how pornography had negative effects on people who watched it.

One day, my secretary leaned her head through the office door and said, "Your noon appointment is here." She then led a well-dressed, middle-aged couple in, and they had a seat. The couple got straight to the point: Their daughter, Courtney, was in her twenties and struggling with sexual sin. After presenting her case, they asked if I would meet with her. I agreed, and we set up an appointment. Courtney was articulate and impressive. After a few rounds of counseling, we traced the root of her issues back to her childhood. As emotions unraveled, she shared that when she was a child, she could not sleep one night and crawled into her parent's bedroom and accidentally saw the pornographic movie they were watching. The images she saw and the subsequent thoughts and emotions she had followed her into her adult life.

A friend of mine once explained that the more he viewed pornography, the more desensitized his mind became to the images. Before long, he had to watch even more depraved acts to achieve the same pleasure, and eventually he found himself fighting off the desire to act out those scenes. Another man argued that his pornography addiction was acceptable because he watched it in private. He reasoned that his actions weren't hurting anyone other than himself. I heard him out and could tell that he genuinely believed what he was saying.

After my friend finished talking, I explained how the pornography industry systematically destroys the fabric of families. I explained how it damages marriages by creating sexual dissatisfaction with a spouse. I shared stories of how X-rated materials often end up in the hands of children who are not emotionally prepared to handle the content and end up becoming addicted at a young age. As I continued to speak, I watched it dawn on him that his actions were not as private as he imagined, that they could have a devastating effect on his family and that they were a part of a global issue affecting every demographic.

Not once has anyone ever told me that an affair benefited his or her life, but I've lost count of how many times infidelity has destroyed someone's family. A man named Roger left a note beside his Bible in the church office and another note on the kitchen table at home, both explaining why he was abandoning his family and church for a woman he had never met. Later, the truth came out that Roger had met a woman in an online pornography chat room. When he left his family to meet up with this woman, he had no idea that his new relationship would lead to charges and incarceration for physically abusing her child.

It is not rational to walk away from the security of a loving family. Why would a man or woman who once loved their spouse and children abandon everything for a person with whom they have no history? Although I don't have all the answers, I believe that in part it's because their lust overrides their ability to think rationally or responsibly. I've watched colleagues walk away from decades of sexual purity only to end up emotionally shattered, broken, and bitter. King Solomon sums up this topic this way: "Whoever commits adultery with a woman lacks understanding; He *who* does so destroys his own soul" (Proverbs 6:32 NKJV).

If we trace back various addictions, we see that most stem from a lack of spiritual connectivity. That is, addiction creeps in when we attempt to find a place of comfort or refuge apart from our Creator. The enemy of your soul knows how easy it is to attack you through the gift of human sexuality. He twists and perverts what God intends for the pleasure of married couples, and sex becomes a weapon against your soul. When God designed us, he created parameters for taking care of ourselves emotionally, mentally, and physically. When we steer away from that bright path and instead travel shadowy roads, we place ourselves in situations that can lead to captivity.

In the heart of every addict is the desperate question, *How do I find my way back to freedom?* Take Lydia, a young lady of thirty-three who had been married for ten years, who went to her mother for financial help. Shocked at the request, her mother asked, "Why do you need money? Both you and Jeff have good-paying jobs." Lydia burst into tears, "We are about to lose our home because I have lost tens of thousands at the casino. I am addicted to gambling, and I don't know how to stop."

Addiction is a prison, and the first step to being set free is to admit that you have a problem and then allow others to help lead you down the path of freedom. Someone once said, "I would rather go through life sober believing I am an alcoholic than to go through life drunk trying to convince myself that I am not." Although I don't necessarily advise labeling ourselves as something we are not, I understand the heart of this quote. It emphasizes that nothing in life will change until we embrace the truth about ourselves. That involves acknowledging, confessing, and assuming responsibility for one's actions rather than pushing blame onto someone else. Jamie Lee Curtis put it this way: "Recovery is an acceptance that your life is in shambles, and you have to change."[48]

I love how this quote from author and poet Sade Andria Zabala captures the awaking of addiction: "I understood myself only after I destroyed myself. And only in the process of fixing myself, did I know who I was."[49] It's not easy to wake up and realize that addiction has snatched away the things you once loved most. It's also hard to come to grips with because if you have any chance of reclaiming your life or identity, you have to let loose the things that have shaped a false identity. It reminds me of an experience I once had at the rehab center for women at which I teach bi-weekly. To remain in the program, one requirement of the women is that they must attend weekly church services. I was shocked and concerned to learn that a couple of the women had to be escorted out of the building because two men with drug connections showed up to intimidate the women and pressure them into leaving the program prematurely. It took courage for those women to call out these men who threatened to pull them back into captivity, and it illustrates my point that it only takes one inappropriate relationship to snatch freedom right out of your hands.

When I counsel individuals who want to reclaim spiritual, physical, emotional, or psychological freedom, one of the first things I ask them to do is avoid any situation that might trigger their addiction. Addiction triggers are not something you set before you but rather something from which you distance yourself. I ask these individuals to list ways they can prevent access to unhealthy desires. If alcohol is the object of temptation, then they must avoid restaurants or environments that serve it. If gambling is their addiction, then they must avoid casinos or electronic gaming. If pornography is an entrapment, then they should add filtering apps to their phones or computers. It is a proven fact that proximity to temptation increases the risk of failure or relapse.

If you are struggling to find freedom from temptation, burn it. Pour it out. Trash it. Whatever it takes, put space between you and your weakness. Think of temptation as a rotten limb on a tree. The best way to preserve the tree is to cut away that which breeds decay. Stop watering what you don't want to live. In the same way, the addiction must be uprooted, starved, or severed. Jesus gave similar advice for overcoming addiction: "If your right hand causes you to stumble, cut it off and throw it away. It is better for you to lose one part of your body than for your whole body to go into hell" (Matthew 5:30 NIV). Although we don't see people literally dismembering parts of their body, the allegory hits the mark in advising us to remove anything from our lives that would hold us hostage and send our souls to hell.

Gather a support system if you can. I have a friend who wanted freedom from a private addiction but refused to have an accountability partner. His pride got in the way of common sense, and he felt like he could kick the habit on his own. As you can guess, his go-it-alone attitude left him without anywhere to turn, and he relapsed within a matter of months. Walking away from addiction and into freedom is best achieved when we have others who will counsel and support our efforts. I've heard it said that "no one delivers themselves from addiction." I agree that partnering together with a support group provides safety, accountability, and renewed self-confidence. I've met too many who think they are strong enough to make it in their strength, and they relapse the moment temptation surfaces. Check in with friends and colleagues who may appear to have it all together. Sometimes the right questions at the right times crack open the door to freedom.

Recovery from addiction is not easy, but it is possible. Take the story of an alcoholic who sat on the curb, hungover from the night before, listening from the flatbed of his farm truck as a man preached over the radio. The longer the preacher spoke, the more hope-filled the distressed man's heart became. At the end of his sermon, the preacher asked if anyone wanted to accept Jesus and the goodness of the gospel. Slowly, but resolutely the man bowed his head and began to pray. While praying and asking God to change his life, he felt an overwhelming urge to stand up. As he followed his impulse, he immediately realized he was sober and delivered from the bondage of alcohol. The man's name was Judge Lindsey, and he's a personal friend of mine. From that moment forward, alcohol never again touched his lips. The power of the Holy Spirit did for him what he could not do for himself. He was set free from the addiction that held him captive.

Judge Lindsey went on to become a minister and established several churches throughout the United States. And just like in this story, once the Holy Spirit comes alive in our hearts, he empowers us to let go of things that have the power to destroy us. In the book of Romans, Paul shares the idea this way: "If you are living according to the flesh, you must die; but if by the Spirit you are putting to death the deeds of the body, you will live" (Romans 8:13 NASB). The Holy Spirit will help us seal shut traps that are designed to ensnare our hearts and destroy our bodies. Our job is to yield to the voice of the Holy Spirit and follow him into freedom.

Freedom is more than letting loose of a harmful habit. Freedom occurs when our nature recognizes and runs to embrace truth. If you were to take a survey of leaders who have found freedom from addiction, the overwhelming majority would tell you that setting in place preventative measures is a million times easier than walking in and out of the cycles of rehabilitation. Powerful leaders know their influence will be tested not by what they say *yes* to but by the destructive things they say *no* to. The world is looking for leaders who do not get their highs from pressure-released pleasures but from maintaining their integrity and being authentic. I will wrap up this chapter with an anonymous quote that sums up everything we have been discussing: "Recovery didn't open the gates of heaven and let me in. Recovery opened the gates of hell and let me out."

11

Prioritize Your Values

I was surprised when Melissa, a young professional woman, made an appointment to meet me for counseling. From what I knew, she enjoyed a perfect childhood. Her father was a famous spiritual leader, and her mother and siblings seemed kind and loving. To outsiders, her family was picture-perfect. But after hearing her talk for a few minutes, it was clear that her take on her childhood was anything but perfect. In a sarcastic tone, she said, "My father missed my birthdays, volleyball games, and dance recitals because he was out saving the world. Even when he was home, he wasn't present; he was always on the phone, answering emails, or working on his next big project." I gave thought to Melissa's words long after our counseling session ended. I realized that one of life's most destructive sins might be prioritizing our jobs too highly because it robs us of important moments with the people standing right in front of us.

My friend Marcus was a well-known songwriter who enjoyed his craft. He spent so much time carving out lyrics that he forgot to carve out time for his wife. His career became the mistress that stole hours away from his family. His desire to work with A-list vocal artists placed heavy demands on his work schedule, and before long, the sixteen-hour workday became routine. His wife longed for attention and affection; instead, she received flowers, perfume, and other meaningless gifts. After a few years of trying to make it work, his wife finally left and never looked back.

I have another friend who spends so much energy fighting through the workday that he has no strength left to enjoy his family. His wife complains that he doesn't want to talk to her or play with the kids when he comes home. He simply wants to crawl into his recliner and plant himself in front of the big screen. I have heard this same scenario enough times to know that she isn't the only one who has a husband who gives less than half his energy to his home life. One of my favorite quotes on this topic is from Marjorie Pay Hinckley, who wrote, "Home is where you are loved the most and act the worst."[50]

Many successful men and women lose sight of what is important, losing their families to divorce or loved ones to general estrangement. It is easy to let work, ambitions, or financial goals steal time reserved for those we love most. To safeguard our relationships, we need to invest in them daily. Prioritizing our values may not always be easy, but it is a task that pays big dividends in the long run. In a private moment with his followers, Jesus brought up the topic of priorities by asking, "What will you gain, if you own the whole world but destroy yourself?" (Luke 9:25 CEV). It was a gentle reminder that one could have a list of superficial successes but, in the end, lose what is significant.

If I were to ask you to decide between advancement in your career or a deeper relationship with your family, would you choose family or career? If you want to know where your priorities lie, then take a glance at your calendar. Make sure that the grueling workdays are offset by a proportionate number of rest and recovery days. If we are to live emotionally balanced lives, then we need to balance our calendars.

On average, a CEO or network leader works sixty to seventy hours a week. According to MoneyInc.com, leaders like Elon Musk, Richard Branson, and Tim Armstrong claim to sleep an average of six hours per night. Tim Cook, Jeff Bezos, and Jack Dorsey average seven hours, and Indra Nooyi, Sergio Marchionne, and Herb Kelleher, say they obtain only four or five hours of sleep per night. Fashion designer Tom Ford and former US president Donald Trump reportedly get only three to four hours of sleep a night.[51] Individuals like these, who claim to require only a few hours of rest each day, are an anomaly. That doesn't work for most of society. Fatigue is a thief. Lack of rest reduces effectiveness on the job and can make us irritable, which creates fractures within our relationships.

I've learned the hard way that the hours we lose with our family are irreplaceable, and I have watched men weep upon the realization that while they raised a business, a stranger raised their family. A wise leader understands that work time and family time are not to be rivals but complementary. One set of values should underscore the other. The key is to find and maintain a healthy schedule that allows you to be at your best in any given situation.

Children who do not have enough quality interaction with their parents often misbehave to gain attention. Not only do they break the rules, but they also tend to believe that rules and restrictions apply to everyone else except for them. Generally, busy parents give expensive things to their kids as a substitute for quality time, perhaps because they subconsciously think gifts and people are disposable. As these neglected kids grow up, they often become self-absorbed, irresponsible, and rebellious young adults. One may add that they often become easy targets of addiction.

Erwin McManus is the pastor of Mosaic Church in Hollywood, California. It is a megachurch with over ten thousand attendees. During an interview that I watched on a Zoom call, McManus shared a personal story that made me stop and reevaluate some areas of my life. He explained that for years his leadership vision had been ahead of the curve. When his church was rapidly growing, he chose to step out of the ministry for six years to be with his son. During that time, he was able to help his son overcome personal issues. Erwin understood the importance of the question Jesus asked at the beginning of this chapter, "What will you gain, if you own the whole world but destroy yourself?" (Luke 9:25 CEV).

King David was one of the most admired and successful men in biblical history. He didn't minor in success; he wrote the textbook on success. In almost every area of life, David was an overachiever. He played music with such passion that evil spirits responded to his lyrics. As a soldier, David was a legend among his colleagues and a terror to his enemies. When he was king, the nation flourished under his leadership. But David didn't earn rave reviews in every category. When David succeeded, he did so with all of his might; when he failed, he did so with equal passion. His successes and failures created tsunami size waves that would crash against the walls of history for decades to come.

The ripple effect of David's decisions created animosity and hostility within the members of his household. His eldest son Amnon raped his half-sister Tamar, and another son Absalom killed Amnon for shaming her. Adonijah and Absalom wanted more than their father's money; in a script made for the big screen, they created a coup to steal his crown. To sum up his relationships within his family, David succeeded in public and failed in private.

The book of 1 Kings talks about David's relationship with one of his sons this way: "But his father had never once infuriated him by asking, 'Why did you do that?'" (1 Kings 1:6 CSB). As a leader, David helped a nation find its identity, but he never guided his sons in discovering theirs through correction or restraint. It doesn't do us any good to rescue others if those closest to us are drowning.

I imagine many leaders experience regret at the end of their lives when they look back over their successes only to discover that they failed in some way to meet the expectations of their family. Our family's greatest need is to know that our love for them ranks on the top of our priority list. Although there are hundreds of ways of expressing love, the one that resonates most is the gift of time. Consider that the average parent spends almost as much time commuting to work as they do caring for their children. According to the US Bureau of Labor Statistics, on average, parents spend 1.3 hours per day with their children under eighteen and, before COVID restrictions, about 1.2 hours on the road between work and home.[52] We live in a fast-paced culture that competes for and often crushes our family time. If we are to be successful at business and family, we must schedule time together and then safeguard that plan.

Many auspicious leaders have established a ritual of dining together with their families. Although the dining times may fluctuate, the rule is that all members must be present for one meal each day. The idea of a mealtime gathering is an excellent opportunity for conversation and catching up with what has been happening in each one's day. Because the atmosphere is casual and not work-related, family members can focus on being together without outside pressures.

Food and culture writer Michael Pollan says that a family meal "is where we teach our children...to get along in society. We teach them how to share. To take turns. To argue without fighting...The family meal is really the nursery of democracy."[53] Having dinner together as a family adds tremendous benefits and reward that strengthens family ties:

Over the past 20 years, research has shown
what parents have known for a long time:
sharing a fun family meal is good for the
spirit, brain, and health of all family members.
Recent studies link regular family meals with
the kinds of behaviors that parents want for
their children: higher grade-point averages,
resilience, and self-esteem. Additionally, family
meals are linked to lower substance abuse
rates, teen pregnancy, eating disorders, and
depression. We see family dinner as prime time
to nourish ethical thinking, and families are
responding to this.[54]

Although society offers excellent ideas about the family unit, I strongly encourage you to read what the Bible says on the subject. In the book of Deuteronomy, God gave Moses a direction for how parents should shape the minds and character of their children: "Impress [my commandments] on your children. Talk about them when you sit at home and when you walk along the road, when you lie down and when you get up" (Deuteronomy 6:7 NIV).

I also agree with actor Michael J. Fox, who said, "Family is not an important thing. It's everything."[55] For over ten years, my son, Jason, traveled to teach leadership at schools and churches. When his daughters were young, he made sure that his wife and daughters could travel with him during the summer months. As the girls grew older and Jason settled into church leadership, he remained intentional about including his family in every ministry aspect. His professional life did not compete with his family time but instead brought his family closer together.

A line from the movie *Lilo and Stitch* talks about family this way: "*Ohana* means family, and family means no one gets left behind or forgotten."[56] It's vital that we set aside personal time with each of our family members. This personal time means spending uninterrupted moments with others and giving them the space to express their feelings, share their dreams, or relax and enjoy carefree activity. Making time for each other is especially important for couples. I have watched seemingly secure couples divorce because they felt their spouses loved the children or their careers more than them. I recently put marriage into perspective by telling someone, "Before children, it was the two of us. After children, it will be the two of us." One way to make your spouse feel special is to surprise him or her with an unexpected lunch date, a surprise gift, or an unplanned getaway. Marriage doesn't have to lack romance or excitement. It is as exciting as two people want to make it.

A successful businessman was deep in thought when his secretary interrupted him and said, "Your two o'clock appointment is here."

Absorbed in his work, he had not looked at his afternoon schedule. "Send them in," he muttered. In walked his teenage son. "Son, what are you doing here?" he asked.

Timidly, his son responded, "I've been missing you. You've had time for everyone else, but not for me. I decided to make an appointment so we could talk without anyone disturbing us."

The father was stunned. What could he say? Nothing. From that moment on, he made more time for his son and stopped allowing work to interfere with their relationship.

In our culture, it is not uncommon for both parents to work while their children are young. Many families find it necessary to have part-time or full-time nannies. On occasion, the children become more attached to those hired to watch them than they are to their parents. Children may even consider daycare workers as family members. And it is sometimes only after children become overly attached to non-family members that parents feel a twinge of guilt.

Theodor Geisel, also known as Dr. Seuss, wisely said, "Sometimes you will never know the value of a moment until it becomes a memory."[57] Children will never forget the moments you spend with them. Vacations are valuable times of intimacy that pull families together and create memories long after the cares of the world are forgotten. That is why families need to spend time together without the intrusion of electronic devices or other distractions that would keep them from leaning in and listening to what others say.

Throughout America and across the globe, family-owned businesses sustain the economy. They dominate the marketplace, with some analysts estimating that up to 90 percent of businesses in the world may be family owned.[58] Keeping businesses within the family allows parents, children, and siblings to journey through life together in unique ways. It empowers family members to figure out ways to work together to achieve shared goals. It unifies the family structure by forging a deep resolve to place the family's needs ahead of individual aspirations. It is an emotional and philosophical learning curve for everyone involved. Without a doubt, this type of venture develops a deep level of commitment that declares, "Live, or die, sink or swim, together we will build a successful business or organization."

It is this type of cohesion that fosters honor, creates transparency, and develops unique ways to resolve conflict. Another advantage of growing a family business is that it allows future generations to carry out the vision. Johnson and Johnson, Ford, Heinz, Gerber, Hershey are just a few examples of companies and organizations representing the family name. Former first lady Barbara Bush captured this thought by saying, "When all the dust is settled and all the crowds are gone, the things that matter are faith, family, and friends."[59]

That is not to say that family businesses are immune to their own set of challenges. Some families have a disabled child, a rebellious teenager, a child who is the target of bullying, a spouse with an addiction, acts of betrayal, or other injustices or burdens that are too difficult to imagine. How we work through these issues reveals our character and ability to show compassion.

Dave Thomas, founder of Wendy's restaurant chain, never knew his biological mother. He was adopted soon after his birth, but his adoptive mother died when he was five, so he went to live with his hard-working adoptive grandmother. Years later, after achieving success in the restaurant business, he formed

The Dave Thomas Foundation for Adoption. Dave worked for the passage of legislation to provide tax credits for parents who adopt foster children.[60]

Someone else who used her passion to bring good to others was former first lady Betty Ford. She created the Betty Ford Center after conquering her addiction to alcohol and prescription pain-killers. Few would imagine that the wife of a US president would come forward with her story of addiction. However, she not only made her issues public, but she also used her story to affect future generations positively. In 1999, President George H.W. Bush awarded Betty Ford the Congressional Gold Medal in honor of her contributions to helping those struggling with addiction.[61]

Other examples of individuals who turned family tragedy into something triumphant include Sharon Hughes, who formed the DOTS (Daughters of the Other Side) to assist others who, like she, survived childhood abuse; and Joe Butler, whose organization, Ability Tree, helps families like his whose lives are impacted by disability. There are numerous stories of leaders who have experienced struggles within their families and have chosen to respond to them in life-giving ways.

Winston Churchill said, "There is no doubt that it is around the family and the home that all the greatest virtues, the most dominating virtues of human society, are created, strengthened and maintained."[62] Just as a grain of sand irritates the oyster to produce a pearl, the private struggles of life can round out our most significant virtues. In the book of Proverbs, King Solomon wrote, "A good name is more desirable than great riches; to be esteemed is better than silver or gold" (Proverbs 22:1 NIV).

Wisdom will ensure riches, but to leave a respected family name is our greatest legacy.

As leaders, our influence has a profound impact on future generations. A study conducted by A. E. Winship compared the legacy of Jonathan Edwards and Max Jukes. Edwards, who lived in the 1700s, was a Puritan minister and became president of Princeton College. Every day Edwards would spend an hour talking with his eleven children and then praying over and blessing them. In comparison, Jukes, who lived during the same time as Edwards, engaged in criminal behavior.

When sociologist Richard L. Dugdale traced both Edwards' and Jukes' legacy, he discovered the following information: Jonathan Edwards' legacy includes: "1 U.S. Vice-President, 1 Dean of a law school, 1 dean of a medical school, 3 U.S. Senators, 3 governors, 3 mayors, 13 college presidents, 30 judges, 60 doctors, 65 professors, 75 military officers, 80 public office holders, 100 lawyers, 100 clergymen, and 285 college graduates." On the other hand, Jukes' family tree included: "7 murderers, 60 thieves, 190 prostitutes, 150 other convicts, 310 paupers, and 440 who were physically wrecked by addiction to alcohol. Of the 1,200 descendants that were studied, 300 died prematurely."[63]

No record indicates that Jukes made any effort to improve his life or the lives of his children. In contrast, Edwards was intentional with his family's future. As a result, he left behind an incredible legacy. Our legacies are greatly influenced by the efforts we take in shaping future generations.

12

Embrace Your Humanity

Suspenseful movies such as *Castaway, I Am Legend, Eight Below,* and *Wrecked* keep viewers on the edge of their seats. As gripping as these storylines may be, they are not nearly as dramatic as the epic story of Noah and the flood. If we squeezed the real-life story into a plotline, it might read, "Family of eight survives global flood and starts new world order."

Recently my wife and I vacationed in Grant County, Kentucky. Although Grant County may not make Google's top ten list of places to visit, it ranked high on mine. It was in this out-of-the-way destination that we visited Ark Encounter and toured a full-size replica of Noah's ark. As I walked through the massive structure, I imagined what it would have been like to be Noah. Later that evening I flipped through passages that highlighted Noah's life and learned that he lived during a time of violence and lawlessness. One passage in Genesis 6 revealed how God became sorrowful for having created man when he saw the wickedness that took place in Noah's generation.

The more I read about Noah, the more I considered the emotional and physical stressors he must have endured to carry out God's instructions. Imagine the weight of knowing God planned to destroy the earth. On top of that weight, add the responsibility of carrying out a divine blueprint designed to save your family from coming judgment. I'm not sure that most of us would be comfortable with such a revelation. Honestly, I'm not convinced that Noah was at ease with the assignment either.

I cannot begin to imagine the physical strength and endurance that Noah and his sons expended constructing a vessel that measured 450 feet long by seventy-five feet wide, standing forty-five feet high. The boat was three stories tall, and the displacement of the ship was 43,300 tons.[64] Anyone familiar with construction or architecture knows that to build a boat this size without the assistance of modern machinery was nothing short of a miracle. And it took more than strength to pull off this feat. It would be 120 years before Noah would hammer the final nail in place. While building it, I am sure he endured public harassment. Friends laughed at him, no doubt. They must have called him names, and not the kind you want others repeating in public. If you have ever found yourself trying to work out God's plan for your life in public, then you might understand Noah's plight.

As I roamed around the ark and stared at the massive beams, I imagined Noah attempting to calculate the amounts of food and water he would need to sustain the animals on board. Remember, he had no clue how long it would be before the waters receded. Imagine trying to pack a suitcase for an international voyage without having a return date.

Once inside the ark, the sounds of the storm had to be horrifying: torrential rain, cracks of lightning, forceful winds, and booming thunder. And the ship's constant swaying with the rising and falling waves must have been unnerving if not altogether nauseating. How all eight passengers pushed beyond their fears and held their emotions together is beyond me.

If you have experienced a season in which you were uncertain of how things would turn out, then you can imagine the kinds of questions that whirled inside Noah's mind. He had to force out dizzying thoughts and worries of potential leaks, cracks, and structural damage. If we played the epic storm out on the big screen in real time, then the viewing audience would have to claw at their seats for 377 days. More than a year passed between the time that Noah's family boarded the ark and the day they climbed out of it, ushering in a new world.

Most biblical movies close with a scene of Noah and his family exiting the ark beneath a rainbow, but the real-life ending would likely reveal the carnage left behind post-flood. It must have been eerie to walk off the ark, knowing no other human life remained. Some theorists believe that if the population rate before the flood was equal to the growth rate in the year 2000, it could have been 750 million people that perished.[65] It would require a great deal of adaptability for Noah to pull his family together and move forward into the unknown.

A scuba diver familiar with traversing off into the deep understands the risks of venturing into the unknown. If a diver descends too quickly, pressure around the ear can create vertigo, and the diver can lose all sense of direction and drown. Trained divers understand the importance of keeping their emotions in check. If emotions escalate and panic sets in, the stress can cause the diver to breathe rapidly instead of slowly and deeply. But if the diver remains calm and adapts to the environment, the oxygen supply to the lungs, brain, and inner ear will regulate. Before long, the vertigo will cease, and the diver can gather his or her bearings.

Like scuba divers, leaders who face unexpected pressures must learn to stay calm when everything inside them wants to panic. Adaptability equals survival. The willingness to remain calm and gather our sense of direction can mean the difference between life and death. Noah had to gather his bearings and lead his family into a strange new world in which he had the monumental tasks of reestablishing a government and a new world order. The previous way of doing things was gone. Now he had to work out the parameters of what the new normal would look like.

The book of Genesis records that Noah's first action after emerging from the ark was to build an altar and worship the Lord. Then he got to work. The first thing to do in the new world was to plant a vineyard. The writer of Genesis puts it this way: "Noah began to be a man of the soil, and he planted a vineyard. He drank of the wine and became drunk and lay uncovered in his tent" (Genesis 9:21 ESV).

We'll never know if Noah became drunk on purpose. In his defense, he lacked the necessary refrigeration to prevent the juice from fermenting, so perhaps it was an innocent mistake. Whether he drank too much on purpose or not, the text says that he was found in an inebriated state, naked in his tent. In Noah's day, his tent was his personal dwelling, where he should have experienced privacy and freedom to exist without ridicule. Unfortunately, Noah's mishap was discovered and then scandalized by his son: "Ham, the father of Canaan, saw the nakedness of his father and told his two brothers outside" (Genesis 9:22 ESV). Knowing his father was drunk was one thing. Staring at his father's exposed body is another. If Ham were a man of honor, he would have stepped out of the tent the moment he saw his father uncovered. He pushed the envelope even further when he spread the news to his siblings. When Ham told the world about his father's indiscretions, he opened the door and allowed dishonor to creep in.

If you have ever caught your parents making a mess of things, then you know how easy it is to spread the news around to your siblings. That kind of tale-bearing is easy to understand in the western world but is frowned upon in other cultures. To the ancients, seeing one's father naked was a violation of civility. It was considered mockery to see the patriarch of the family uncovered. In the modern-day, it would be equivalent to having one of our teens publicize our mistakes on social media. As ridiculous as it may seem to younger generations, those kinds of actions in Noah's day warranted extreme punishment, including the death penalty.

When Ham told his brothers what he saw, they did the noble thing: "Shem and Japheth took a garment, laid it on both their shoulders and walked backward and covered the nakedness of their father. Their faces were turned backward, and they did not see their father's nakedness" (Genesis 9:23 ESV). They didn't want to see their father's failures, nor did they want anyone else to see them. It is noble when sons secretly safeguard their fathers.

In biblical days, the patriarch, or leader, had the authority to bless or curse those who dishonored him. Noah understood that right and took action when he awakened from his inebriated condition: "When Noah awoke from his wine and knew what his youngest son had done to him, he said, 'Cursed be Canaan; a servant of servants shall he be to his brothers.' He also said, 'Blessed be the Lord, the God of Shem; and let Canaan be his servant. May God enlarge Japheth, and let him dwell in the tents of Shem, and let Canaan be his servant'" (Genesis 9:24–27 ESV).

If you follow the story of this family, you will see that the curse over Ham's life went generations deep. The *curse* spoken by Noah didn't stop with Ham but fell also on his youngest son, Canaan. If we dig a little deeper, we could tie together that Ham was the youngest son of Noah and Canaan was Ham's youngest son. Canaan's legacy would go deep into sexual perversion and idol worship and oppose those who served God. Over time Canaan's sons would become servants to his brothers, who had lavished their father with honor.

Unlike the curse pronounced on Canaan, Noah spoke a blessing over Shem and Japheth. The blessing included verbal affirmation that their families would be enlarged and prosperous. If you like Jewish history, then it is worth noting that we can trace Shem's legacy to Abraham. Honor determined the destiny of three sons. It still determines the future of sons today.

Have you ever wondered how children raised in the same household by the same parents turn out so differently? I've considered this question and have landed on this idea: The future of the child is determined by whether he or she shows honor or dishonor to their parents. If you have studied the life of David, then you know one of his greatest attributes was his willingness to keep family matters quiet. On more than one occasion, David remained silent when he could have criticized. Even when his father-in-law Saul tried to kill him, David remained peaceful and calm. To make a rather long story short, while searching for David, King Saul went into a cave to relieve himself. As fate would have it, that cave was the very one David and his men were hiding in. Rather than taking this opportunity to expose or belittle his father-in-law, David covered Saul's tracks.

As with most followers, David's men didn't understand why their leader allowed Saul to slip out of an embarrassing situation. In another encounter, David's men tried to convince him to give one of them clearance to kill Saul. If you read the remainder of the story in 1 Samuel 24, you will see how David cried out from a distance to let Saul know that he looked past his vulnerability. If you keep winding your way through their saga, Saul's last chapter in 1 Samuel 31 ends with his suicide. When a man saw what happened to Saul, he ran and told David. As the words tumbled out of the messenger's mouth, David orders the messenger to be killed. Why? Because David understood that even a crazed king needed to be covered. Honor demands we not touch or come against those God has anointed.

Disclosure of private information will often separate relationships and bring division between trusted friends. The wise King Solomon offered good advice about gossip: "He who repeats a matter separates close friends" (Proverbs 17:9 ESV). Another way to think about this is that once we make something public, the wind carries off our words. Loosely spoken words often create damage that we can never repair. I've watched too many families and churches fall apart over a few sentences spoken in a defamatory way.

Over the years, countless leaders have complained to me that their homes aren't a place of celebration but centers for criticism. Home should be the place where a leader feels understood the most and confident that their faults are seen but kept private. But far too often, those closest to us concentrate on our weaknesses without ever recognizing the wealth within us. What happens in the privacy of our home should be off-limits to the public. Leaders shouldn't have to live in glass houses.

I've had middle-aged men confess that they were on the verge of walking away from high profile careers not because they couldn't handle the pressure of the job but because they couldn't handle the pressures of living in the public eye. They were publicly called out if they owned a nice car, enjoyed an expensive vacation, or wore brand-name clothing. Few things cripple a leader's confidence more than superficial criticism, and the public will criticize you at every turn.

Admittedly, it is easy to forget the human side of leaders, many of whom lie awake at night and replay their failures in their heads. If you were to Google search a list of biblical leaders who limped away from their letdowns, you would amass a significant number of names. Jonah, who led a city to repentance and then fought depression, would top the list. I'm sure David spent many hours lamenting that he plotted out the execution of his new wife's husband. Peter probably cursed when he remembered standing by while soldiers took away the Savior. Although these men had to face their mistakes, they also acknowledged that their failures wouldn't have the final word. They picked up the pieces and made something memorable out of their messes.

Running throughout this book is a theme that encourages leaders to be open, transparent, and authentic. Biblical giants like Noah, King Saul, King David, Isaiah, Simon Peter, and John Mark illustrate the importance of living life authentically. Though they each lived very different lives, the one thing they had in common was that God pulled the covers off their secrets to heal them. In a profound moment, Jesus reminded his disciples to "Watch and pray so that you will not fall into temptation. The spirit is willing, but the flesh is weak" (Matthew 26:41 NIV). He was emphasizing that prayer is a buffer that puts distance between temptations and our nature. The closer we are to God, the more we realize our weaknesses and the more we rely on the Holy Spirit to help us lead holy lives. Romans 8:26 reveals that "the Spirit helps us in our weakness" (NIV).

Rev. Jesse Jackson shared the following story at the Democratic National Convention in 1992, and it stuck in my mind:

> Not very long ago I was in South Carolina speaking to a small school. I saw a strange and unusual sight. I saw a six-foot-eight athlete walking across the campus, holding the hand of a three-foot dwarf. There was this contrast. It looked to be romantic. She was looking up, and he was looking down. They got to where the sidewalks crossed, and she jumped up on the bench, and they embraced and kissed. And he gave her her books. She went skipping down the sidewalks. I tried to act normal, but… it looked funny to me. I said, "Mr. President, what am I looking at?" He said, "Well, I thought you would ask. You see, that is his sister. As a matter of fact, it is his twin sister. And by some freak of genetics, he came out the giant, she came out the dwarf. He's a top athlete in this state. We couldn't afford to get him. All the big schools offered him scholarships. The pros offered him a contract. But he said, 'I can only go to the college that my sister can get a scholarship.'…'But we can't give two scholarships. We have bright lights. We have pro possibilities.' He said, 'But if my sister can't go, I can't go.'"[66]

Like these twins, some of us are born giants, with exceptional abilities, giftedness, and appearances. Others are less fortunate. The heart of the leader wants to elevate the lesser and share with them the opportunity for hope and advancement. If today's leaders are to be effective, then they must be willing to bare their humanity. It takes courage to live transparently, but that vulnerability creates a lifelong connection with others. Our perception of others can make men appear as giants when in reality they are mere mortals. Putting others on a pedestal elevates them to places that are easy to fall from, and their fall isn't usually one of grace or glory.

I thought about one of my childhood heroes, who's a fictional character from another planet. Endowed with superhuman abilities, he could fly, enjoyed extraordinary strength, and possessed X-ray vision. You can probably guess that I am referring to Superman. As remarkable as he was, he also had a human side. When he wasn't busy being Superman, he was journalist Clark Kent. If you watched the TV show or any of the Superman movies, then you know that Clark would often slip into a closet or some other hidden place and emerge moments later as Superman. As a superhero, he was bulletproof, and kryptonite was his only weakness. The slightest contact with the smallest amount of kryptonite stripped him of his superpowers.

Like most boys, I didn't focus on my superhero's weakness but proudly wore a cape with his initial inscribed on the back. When I tied the cape around my neck, I imagined myself flying and enjoying all the powers he possessed. Once I climbed onto a low-lying roof and attempted to fly off. After falling to the ground, I tried to hide the pain and embarrassment of knowing others had seen me fail at trying to be Superman. In retrospect, I should have known Superman wasn't as invincible as he let on. One dead giveaway was the fact that bullets bounced off him, but when a villain swung at him, he always ducked. Superman wasn't immune to sucker punches, and neither are we.

As leaders grow, it becomes easy for them to believe the hype surrounding their reputation. But deep down, every leader is aware that they might get sucker punched. They know their Achilles' heel. Too many leaders try to act like they're invincible and end up falling in the first round of the fight. The truth is that no leader hits a home run every time they swing the bat. Leaders strike out, miss the mark, rip a shot off the green, or come up with empty nets. No one hits the bull's eye every time. Not Superman. Not you.

Along the journey, I have attempted to push beyond teaching leadership principles to addressing the personal issues with which leaders often struggle. We have talked about our attempts to conceal, confront, and take ownership of our weaknesses. In a roundabout kind of way, I believe your weakness may even be the key to your success. I pray that I have helped you accept your flaws. My hope is that you will accept who you are and where you are along this journey. Character flaws, sins, mistakes, personal issues, failures, successes, giftedness, and relationships make you who you are. It is not the similarities with others but the ways you are different that set you apart.

After decades of assisting leaders, I promise you this: We need God, and we need each other. I've also come to know the following:

> This foolish plan of God is wiser than the wisest of human plans, and God's weakness is stronger than the greatest of human strength. Remember, dear brothers and sisters, that few of you were wise in the world's eyes or powerful or wealthy when God called you. Instead, God chose things the world considers foolish in order to shame those who think they are wise. And he chose things that are powerless to shame those who are powerful. (1 Corinthians 1:25–27 NLT)

This passage reveals the hidden truth that God chose to use us, who are powerless, to show his greatness. The apostle Paul, who wrote two-thirds of the New Testament, put it this way:

> I came to you in weakness—timid and trembling. And my message and my preaching were very plain. Rather than using clever and persuasive speeches, I relied only on the power of the Holy Spirit. I did this so you would trust not in human wisdom but in the power of God. (1 Corinthians 2:3–5 NLT)

When we humble ourselves and acknowledge that we need God's help, he in turn elevates us. People will not see us but the Christ who is in us. Paul went on to explain that our weakness is an opportunity for God to display his grace in us: "[The Lord] said to me, 'My grace is sufficient for you, for my power is made perfect in weakness.' Therefore I will boast all the more gladly about my weaknesses, so that Christ's power may rest on me" (2 Corinthians 12:9 NIV).

Now that we can accept and embrace personal weaknesses, we can move forward with newfound freedom. We can square off with the assurance that God will use us right where we are despite our shortcomings. Remember, God will use us in ways we have not imagined if we continually carve out our character. At the heart of a genuine leader is a willingness to be honest with themselves when no one else is looking. It is the ability to look at and love ourselves through the eyes of our Creator.

As we end our journey together, I trust that this book has challenged you to reassess your personal values and priorities, realign your relationships, and restore your heart, which is that of a leader. As you move forward, remember to turn your life lessons into a well of wisdom for yourself and others who follow you. You are a bulletproof leader, and you are free to live with confidence that with God's help, no weapon formed against you shall succeed (Isaiah 54:17 ESV). I will end this book with the words of a skeptic, a persecutor of believers, and a hater of Christ, who was converted and whom God used to preach the gospel of Jesus, Paul the Apostle: "By the grace of God I am what I am, and his grace to me was not without effect. No, I worked harder than all of them—yet not I, but the grace of God that was with me" (1 Corinthians 15:10 NIV).

Endnotes

1   T. J. Auclair, "High School Golfer Calls Penalty on Herself, Loses State Title," PGA (website), June 6, 2018, https://www.pga.com.

2   Peter Economy, "21 Zig Ziglar Quotes to Inspire Your Success in Life and Business," Inc. (website), October 2, 2014, https://www.inc.com.

3   Bill Hybels, *Courageous Leadership* (Grand Rapids: Zondervan, 2002), 189.

4   Joseph McBride, *Steven Spielberg: A Biography* (New York: Simon & Schuster, 1997), 131.

5   TV Mahalingam, "These five business icons got fired before they became legends," The Economic Times, updated March 13, 2015, https://economictimes.indiatimes.com.

6   Joanna L. Grossman, "Vice President Pence's 'Never Dine Alone with a Woman' Rule Isn't Honorable. It's Probably Illegal," Vox (website), updated December 4, 2017, https://www.vox.com.

7   Myles Monroe, *Myles Munroe Devotional & Journal: 365 Days to Realize Your Potential* (Shippensburg, PA: Destiny Image Publishers, 2007).

8   Kalyan B. Bhattacharyya, "Adolf Hitler and His Parkinsonism," *Annals of Indian Academy of Neurology*, vol. 18,4 (2015): 387–90, https://www.ncbi.nlm.nih.gov.

9   Froot Group, "Ministry Hopping," Ministry Jobs (website), September 13, 2017, https://ministryjobs.com.

10 Joel Sherman, "MLB Should Let Others Decide Pete Rose's Hall of Fame Case," *New York Post* (website), February 5, 2020, https://nypost.com.

11 Aric Jenkins, "The Deadliest U.S. Bridge Collapses Over the Past 50 Years," *Time* (website), March 31, 2017, https://time.com.

12 "Muhammad Ali Quotes," BrainyQuote.com (website), BrainyMedia Inc, accessed October 28, 2021, https://www.brainyquote.com.

13 The Beatles, *The Beatles Anthology*, (San Francisco: Chronicle Books, 2000), 10.

14 Magdalena Podobińska, "Power of Teachers' Words: The Influence on Pupils' Grades and Behaviour," *World Scientific News* 77(1) (2017), 1–106, http://www.worldscientificnews.com.

15 Gillian Bethel, "Jacob the Supplanter," Hartland (website), July 19, 2017, https://hartland.edu.

16 Elian Peltier and Anna Codrea-Rado, "French Museum Discovers More Than Half Its Collection Is Fake," *The New York Times* (website), April 30, 2018, https://www.nytimes.com.

17   John Addison, "5 Bold Leadership Qualities of Dwight D. Eisenhower (Updated)," Addison Leadership (website), September 15, 2021, https://johnaddisonleadership.com.

18   Evan Thomas, "The Brilliant Prudence of Dwight Eisenhower," The Atlantic (website), September 19, 2012, https://www.theatlantic.com.

19   Stelman Smith and Judson Cornwall, *The Exhaustive Dictionary of Bible Names*, (Alachua, FL: Bridge-Logos, 1998), 128.

20   "Snapped: The moment Steven Bradbury skated to Olympic immortality," Olympics.com, January 24, 2019, https://olympics.com.

21   "Quote by Zig Ziglar," Goodreads (website), Goodreads, Inc., accessed October 28, 2021, https://www.goodreads.com.

22   A.J. "The Sauce" Dillon (@ajdillon7), "Whoever counted me out simply can't count," January 21, 2019, 8:16 p.m., https://twitter.com.

23   Tom Wilmoth, "A Message of Success," *RenewANation* (website), accessed July 30, 2021, https://www.renewanation.org.

24   Scott Cohn, "10 Years Later, Here's What Became of Bernie Madoff's Inner Circle," CNBC (website), December 10, 2018, https://www.cnbc.com.

25   Samuel R. Chand, *Cracking Your Church's Culture Code: Seven Keys to Unleashing Vision and Inspiration*, (San Francisco: Jossey-Bass, 2011).

26   Dan Rather, "Vince Gill," AXS TV (website), 2015, https:// www.axs.tv.

27   Patrick Gillespie, "Netflix CEO: I Take 6 Weeks of Vacation Each Year," CNN (website), November 3, 2015, https:// money.cnn.com.

28   Benjamin Snyder, "How Richard Branson and 5 Other CEOs Get Ahead by Scheduling Time Off," CNBC.com, April 29, 2017, https://www.cnbc.com.

29   "9 Successful People Who Prove You Should Use Your Vacation Time," *HuffPost*, December 6, 2017, https://www. huffpost.com.

30   "13 Stats on Mental Health and the Church," Lifeway Research (website), May 1, 2018, https://lifewayresearch. com.

31   "Mental Health Awareness," Good Samaritan Project (website), accessed October 28, 2021, https:// goodsamaritanproject.net.

32   "He helped us with our feelings," Mister Rogers' Neighborhood (website), accessed October 28, 2021, https://www.misterrogers.org.

33   Summer Anderson, "How Leaders Can Battle Depression and Overcome the Condition," StartUp Mindset (website), 2017, https://startupmindset.com.

34   Dictionary.com, s.v. "depression," accessed July 26, 2021, https://www.dictionary.com.

35 Sonja, Aalbers, Laura Fusary-Poli, et al., "Music Therapy for Depression," Healthy People 2030 (website), Office of Disease Prevention and Health Promotion, February 28, 2018, https://www.healthypeople.gov.

36 Wikipedia contributors, "Elijah," *Wikipedia, The Free Encyclopedia*, updated July 26, 2021, https://en.wikipedia.org.

37 Neel Burton, MD, "Depressive Realism: Wisdom or Madness?," Psychology Today (website), June 5, 2012, https://www.psychologytoday.com.

38 Joshua Wolf Shenk, "Lincoln's Great Depression," *The Atlantic* (website), October 2005, https://www.theatlantic.com.

39 "If You Can't Fly, Then Run," Literary Devices (website), accessed October 28, 2021, https://literarydevices.net.

40 John Kuriski, "12 Historic Leaders Who Struggled with Mental Illness," *All That's Interesting* (website), updated February 10, 2017, https://allthatsinteresting.com.

41 "Quote by Beau Taplin," Goodreads (website), Goodreads, Inc., accessed October 28, 2021, https://www.goodreads.com.

42 "Quote by J.M. Storm," Goodreads (website), Goodreads, Inc., accessed October 28, 2021, https://www.goodreads.com.

43 "Nearly One in Three People Know Someone Addicted to Opioids; More than Half of Millennials believe it is Easy to Get Illegal Opioids," American Psychiatric Association (website), May 7, 2018, https://www.psychiatry.org.

44 Allana Akhtar, "7 Business Leaders Who Are Completely Open about Their Struggles with Alcohol and Drugs," *Insider* (website), December 8, 2019, https://www.businessinsider.com.

45 "Addictive Personality," AlcoholRehab.com, American Addiction Centers, October 9, 2020, https://alcoholrehab.com.

46 "The Leadership Survey on Pastors and Internet Pornography," Christianity Today (website), accessed October 28, 2021, https://www.christianitytoday.com.

47 "Big Porn: Porn Industry Revealed," Culture Reframed (website), October 2, 2019, https://www.culturereframed.org.

48 "Addiction Recovery: The Best 55 Sayings And Recovery Quotes," Steps Recovery Centers (website), accessed October 29, 2021, https://www.stepsrc.com.

49 "Quote by Sade Andria Zabala," Goodreads (website), Goodreads, Inc., accessed October 29, 2021, https://www.goodreads.com.

50 "Quote by Marjorie Pay Hinckley," Goodreads (website), Goodreads, Inc., accessed October 29, 2021, https://www.goodreads.com.

51 Erin Berman, "How Much Sleep Should a CEO Get?" MoneyInc. (website), April 24, 2018, https://moneyinc.com.

52 "American Time Use Survey Summary," U.S. Bureau of
    Labor Statistics (website), United States Department of
    Labor, July 22, 2021, https://www.bls.gov.

53 Richard Johnson, "Michael Pollan Says the Family Meal is
    the Nursery of Democracy," Gulf News (website), June 6,
    2013, https://gulfnews.com.

54 "The Family Dinner Project," Project Zero (website),
    Harvard Graduate School of Education, accessed July 31,
    2021, http://www.pz.harvard.edu.

55 "Michael J. Fox—Quotes," IMDb (website), IMDb.com,
    Inc., accessed October 29, 2021, https://m.imdb.com.

56 *Lilo and Stitch*, directed by Chris Sanders and Dean
    DeBlois, 2002, Walt Disney Pictures, 85 minutes.

57 "Sometimes you will never know the value of a moment,
    until it becomes a memory.," Quotespedia (website),
    accessed October 29, 2021, https://www.quotespedia.org.

58 "Knowledge into Action: Preparing the Next Generation of
    Family Business Leaders," Cornell SC Johnson College of
    Business (website), April 28, 2020, https://business.cornell.
    edu.

59 Pat Ralph, "12 quotes that show why Barbara Bush was
    such a beloved first lady," Business Insider India (website),
    April 18, 2018, https://www.businessinsider.com.

60 John Tucker, "The Inspirational Story of Wendy's Founder
    Dave Thomas," Nav (website), July 23, 2018, https://www.
    nav.com.

61 "Betty Ford," Biography (website), updated May 11, 2020, https://www.biography.com.

62 "Quote by Winston S. Churchill," Goodreads (website), Goodreads, Inc., accessed October 29, 2021, https://www. goodreads.com.

63 Larry Ballard, "Multigenerational Legacies—the Story of Jonathan Edwards," Family Ministries: Youth with a Mission, July 1, 2017, https://www.ywam-fmi.org.

64 Merrill F. Unger, *Archaeology and the Old Testament*, (Grand Rapids: Zondervan Publishing House, 1954), 59–60.

65 "What Was the Pre-Flood Population Like?," Answers in Genesis (website), January 6, 2016, https:// answersingenesis.org.

66 "Hope for American Domestic Problems," C-SPAN (website), July 14, 1992, https://www.c-span.org.

About the Author

Glenn Dorsey is a renowned leader, international conference speaker, author, and pastor. He travels to diverse, cross-cultural groups throughout America and internationally, including Africa, Europe, India, and Micronesia. He conducts annual conferences in the United States called Gear Up Conference, which is designed to equip and train young leaders, and Elevate Conference for individuals in need of emotional healing. Glenn has served as the visionary leader of School of Urban Missions (SUM), a four-year curriculum offering master and doctorate-level education. He is also the founder and president of Glenn Dorsey Ministries, Inc.

Whether speaking to corporate or community leaders, pastors, or international dignitaries, Glenn's love and passion for developing leaders from the inside out make his messages relevant and robust. As a veteran pastor for over forty-four years and president of the Ministerial Alliance, Glenn understands what it takes to reach, develop, and change the heart of a leader.

Glenn has authored other books, including *Out of the Snare, Pain Free,* and *Father Me*, which are in circulation worldwide and have been translated into French and Romanian. *Father Me,* a book bringing reconciliation to fathers and children, has been incorporated into the Arkansas Better Days statewide curriculum upon request. *Out of the Snare* and *Pain Free* are currently used in many faith-based rehabilitation centers to help bring healing to those who have been traumatized and oppressed.

Along with speaking and writing, Glenn has appeared on media outlets such as *TBN, Alive TV, Lamb Broadcasting, WATC-TV,* a host of radio affiliates, and online broadcasts. He was also awarded the Key to the City of Beebe, Arkansas, by the mayor on two occasions.

An avid golfer who also enjoys hunting and fishing, Glenn and his wife, Gladys, have been married for more than fifty years and have two children and five grandchildren.